M O N E Y anfwers

OR, AN

E S S A Y

TO MAKE

M O N E Y

Sufficiently plentiful

Amongft all Ranks of PEOPLE,

AND

Increafe our Foreign and Domeftick TRADE;
Fill the EMPTY HOUSES with Inhabitants,

Encourage the MARRIAGE STATE,

Leffen the

Number of HAWKERS and PEDLARS,

A N D,

In a great meafure, prevent giving long CRE-
DIT, and making bad DEBTS in TRADE.

Likewife fhewing,

The Abfurdity of going to War about TRADE ;
and the moft likely Method to prevent the Clandeftine
Exportation of our WOOL:

A N D A L S O

To reduce the NATIONAL DEBTS, and eafe
the T A X E S.

By J ACOB VANDERLINT.

The Deftruction of the Poor is their Poverty. Prov. x. 15.

L O N D O N :

Printed for T. Cox; and Sold by J. WILFORD, at the *Three*
Flower de Luces behind the *Chapter-Houfe* in St. *Paul's-Church-*
Yard. M.DCC.XXXIV.   [Price 1 s. 6d.]

The Lord Baltimore Press
BALTIMORE, MD., U. S. A.

TO THE

Merchants of *Great-Britain.*

Gentlemen,

F this Essay be, what I humbly presume it is, an evident and clear Account of the Foundation of the Trade of the World; and so particularly adapted to the State of Trade in this Nation, as to point out the Means to inlarge, and carry it to the utmost Perfection; I think, I may reasonably hope that, as it must merit your Regard, so it will not be unworthy your Patronage.

But this is not the only Motive, which induces me most humbly to dedicate it to you, Gentlemen: No; I have the Interest and Advancement of Trade (on which the Welfare and Happiness of Mankind so much depends) really at Heart. And therefore (being sensible ‖ the Flaws and Imperfections of this Work can't escape your Penetration) would earnestly recommend it to your Improvement: That the great Basis of Trade may be establish'd by Principles, as solid and perspicuous, as those Rules by which your particular Affairs are directed. And then it will be no greater Difficulty to account for the Changes and Turns the Trade of Nations takes, than it is, by your exact and excellent Method of

8 Dedication

Accounts, to shew all the Turns any of your particular Affairs take. And I am well satisfied, the former, by my Principles, when improv'd by your refin'd Judgment and Skill in Trade, will be as easy and demonstrative as the latter. I am, with the greatest Esteem,

G E N T L E M E N,

Your most humble Servant,

Jacob Vanderlint.

PREFACE.

EDUCING the present Rates of Labour, appears to me so absolutely necessary to increase our foreign and domestick Trade, that I have endeavour'd to shew how it may be effected, to the great Advantage of every Person, from the highest to the lowest, in the Community; and that reducing the Rates of Labour, the Way propos'd in this Essay, which is the only Way it can possibly be done, will together with it effect all the Things I have mentioned in the Title Page; and this Method will cause Multitudes to become the Owners and Possessors of Property, who otherwise never will have a Shilling to spare.

I am sorry I am not, in all Respects, equal to this most important Undertaking; yet I doubt not, that I have suf ‖ ficiently made out what I have under- taken; and though not with the Accuracy and Conciseness of a Scholar, yet with that Perspicuity and Evidence which may be expected from an ordinary Tradesman.

And as this is the utmost I am capable of, I hope the Inaccuracy and Prolixity of this Performance will be overlooked by the candid and ingenuous Reader, for the Sake of the Importance of the Subject, and that Evidence with which I have supported my

Arguments. And I the rather hope for this Indulgence, since the Path I tread is not only unfrequented, but perhaps entirely new: And as the Principles of Trade, I proceed on, are founded in the Nature of Things, and Constitution of the World itself, so I doubt not that they are capable of strict Demonstration, in which Way I should be glad to see them handled by such as have Abilities for it.

AN

ESSAY

To make MONEY fufficiently plentiful amongft all Ranks of People, &c.

HE bad Circumstances Trade in general hath been in for some Time, which instead of mending seems still growing worse, induced me to consider the Causes, which the sudden and extraordinary Rise of Victuals a few Years ago did, in my Opinion, clearly enough point out and discover. For I observed, that Rise was not intirely owing to the Seasons, which will always influence the Price of Necessaries; but rather, and indeed chiefly, to the Want of Cultivating and Tilling a great deal more Land, to make the Plenty greater: And as the Rise of any Thing implies some Degree of Scarcity, so this suggests that too few of ‖ the People are 2 imploy'd in Cultivation of Land, and the Affairs

thereof, and consequently too many in all Trades, Manufactures, and Professions; whence these being thus overstock'd with Numbers, must needs be depressed and embarrassed; as they certainly are, in Reference to the great End of them, which is solely Profit; whilst the other wants the Surplusage of Hands to increase the Plenty, and keep down the Price of Necessaries from rising as they did at that Time.

In Consequence of these general Observations, I have since made many Reflections, which I hope may be useful; and therefore have endeavour'd to write some of them down, that it may clearly appear where the Fault lies, and how it may be remedied; and I trust I have sufficiently done this in the following Essay.

And as I find, Considerations on the Use, Necessity, Increase, and Diminution of Money amongst the People, will best explain this momentous Affair; I shall lay down and illustrate some Principles relating to Money, which I think deserve to be regarded as Maxims.

I. Money (*i. e.* Gold and Silver) being, by the Consent of all Nations, become Counters for adjusting the Value of all Things else, and balancing all Accounts between Man and Man; and the Means by which Commodities of all Kinds are procured and transferred from one to another; is hence become the sole Medium of Trade.

II. Money (by which understand always Gold and Silver) can be brought into a Nation, that hath not ₃Mines, by this Means only; *viz.* ‖ by such Nation's exporting more Goods in Value than they import: For, in Proportion, as the Value of the Exports exceeds the Value of the Imports, Money, which must balance the Account, increaseth faster or

slower; and, contrariwise, where the Imports exceed
the Value of the Exports, the Cash of such Nation
must proportionably diminish. And this is called,
and doth constitute, the general Balance of the
Trade of all Nations, that have not Mines.

III. Money will be most plentiful, where the Mines
are: I mean by this, just the same as if I should say
the Quantity of Coals will be greater at *Newcastle*
than at any Place that is supplied only with Coals
from thence: And consequently I mean that Gold
and Silver will as certainly be less valuable where
the Mines are, than at any other Place which is supplied with those Metals by them; as Coals are, and
will be less valuable at *Newcastle*, than at any other
Place that is supplied with Coals only from thence.
Whence it follows,

IV. That the Prices of the Produce or Manufactures of every Nation will be higher or lower, according as the Quantity of Cash circulating in such Nation is greater or less, in Proportion to the Number
of People inhabiting such Nation.

To illustrate this, let it be supposed that we have
ten Millions of Cash, and as many People in *England*; it's evident they have twice as much Money
amongst them, in Proportion to their Number, as
they wou'd have if their Number were doubled, and
the Quantity of ‖ Cash remain'd just the same.4
And therefore, I think, they could give but half the
Price for Things in general in this Case, that they
could do when they were but half the Number, with
the same Quantity of Money circulating and divided
amongst them. Wherefore, if the People increase,
and the Cash doth not increase in like Proportion,
the Prices of Things must fall; for all the People
must have Necessaries, to procure which they must
all have Money: This will divide the same Quantity

of Cash into more Parts, that is, lessen the Parts; and then it's evident they can't pay so much for their Necessaries, as when the same Cash divided into fewer Parts, makes the Parts greater.

The Prices of all Things in this Kingdom, some Centuries ago, were vastly lower than they are now. In the Reign of King *Henry the Eighth*, it was enacted, that Butchers should sell their Meat by Weight; Beef at an Half-penny, and Mutton at Three-farthings *per* Pound: And if we look back to the Reign of King *Edward the Third*, we find Wheat was sold at two Shillings *per* Quarter, a fat Ox for a Noble, a fat Sheep for Six-pence, six Pidgeons for a Penny, a fat Goose for Two-pence, a Pig for a Penny; and other Things in Proportion. See *Baker's Chronicle*.[1]

Now, since the great Difference of the Prices of these Things now, to what they then sold for, is undoubtedly owing solely to the great Quantity of Gold and Silver, which since that Time hath been brought into this Kingdom by Trade, which hath furnished us with so much more Money, to pay such 5 a vast deal ‖ more as we now must, and do give for them; it follows, that the Prices of Things will certainly rise in every Nation, as the Gold and Silver increase amongst the People; and, consequently, that where the Gold and Silver decrease in any Nation, the Prices of all Things must fall proportionably to such Decrease of Money, or the People must be distress'd; unless the Number of People decrease in as great Proportion as the Cash decreaseth in any such Nation.

V. Banking, so far as one is paid with the Money of another, that is, where more Cash Notes are circulated, than all the Cash the Bankers are really possessed of will immediately answer and make good; I say, so long as this Credit is maintain'd, it hath the same Effect, as if there was so much more Cash really circulating and divided amongst the People; and will be attended with these Consequences, that as the Price of Things will hence be rais'd, it must and will make us the Market, to receive the Commodities of every Country whose Prices of Things are cheaper than ours. And though we should lay on Duties, or prohibit such Goods, this will not prevent the Mischief, because we shall not be able to carry our Commodities thus raised to any Nation, where Things are cheaper than ours; and because such Nations will hence be enabled to set up many of our Manufactures, &c. and by their Cheapness so interfere in our Trade at all other foreign Markets, as to turn the Balance of Trade against us, which will diminish the Cash of the Nation. The same Thing must || be understood of all publick Securities what-6 ever, that operate as Money amongst us.

VI. The Plenty or Scarcity of any particular Thing, is the sole Cause whence any Commodity or Thing can become higher or lower in Price; or, in other Words, as the Demand is greater or less in Proportion to the Quantity of any Thing, so will such Thing, whatsoever it is, be cheaper or dearer. Nor can any Arts or Laws make this otherwise, any more than Laws or Arts can alter the Nature of Things.

VII. All Things, that are in the World, are the Produce of the Ground originally; and thence must all Things be raised. The more Land therefore shall be improv'd and cultivated, &c. the greater will the Plenty of all Things be, and the more People will it also imploy. And as the Produce will hence be increased, so will the Consumption of all Things increase too; and the greater the Plenty becomes this Way, the cheaper will every Thing be.

And thus will Money become plentiful, because less Money will purchase every Thing, in just the same Proportion as the Plenty of every Thing shall reduce the Prices, by the Increase of every Thing in Respect of the Demand. And if this Method be sufficiently persued, the Plenty may be increased so much as to make Victuals and Drink half the Price that they are at now; which will make the Price of the Labour of Working People much lower; for the Rates of Labour are always settled and constituted of the Price of Victuals and Drink: And all 7 Manufactures will be vastly || cheaper; for the Value of all Manufactures is chiefly constituted of the Price or Charge of the Labour bestowed thereon. This therefore shews how to make Money plentiful, *viz.*

First, By thus making the Necessaries of Life cheaper, to such a Degree as shall be found effectual to reduce the present Rates of Labour, and thereby the Price of every Thing else, so much, that the Money, now circulating amongst the People, may extend a vast deal further than it now will do.

Secondly, We shall hence be enabled to make, and export our Manufactures at much lower Prices; and this must needs cause us to export abundance more of them to those Nations that now take them of us; besides that it will enable us to carry our Produce, *&c.* further and cheaper, to induce other Nations to take them of us, who now perhaps do not take any of our Goods; whence the Cash of the Nation will certainly increase, by raising the Value of our Exports above the Value of our Imports; that is, the Balance of Trade will thus be in our Favour, or Money will thus be made plentiful.

VIII. Plenty of Money never fails to make Trade flourish; because, where Money is plentiful, the People in general are thereby enabled, and will not fail to be as much greater Consumers of every Thing, as such Plenty of Money can make them: Therefore Trade is always found to flourish (*i. e.* increase) as Money grows more plentiful amongst the People. The Year 1720, was a Proof in Fact of this Maxim. And hence the Revenue must needs increase likewise; since the Duties are always || levied on the 8 Things which the People consume and use.

IX. Where Trade flourishes (*i. e.* where the Balance of Trade is considerably in Favour of any Nation) there the People always increase greatly, and become generally happy; whence such Nations ever grow potent and formidable. This hath always been found true in Fact, and is almost self-evident.

X. 'Tis the Strength, Honour, and Interest of every Government, that their Subjects be as numerous, as the Continent they govern will support in an happy Condition; and as the Happiness (*i. e.* the Riches) and Numbers of the Subjects, are greater or less, so will the Strength, Honour, and Revenue of every Government be greater or less.

XI. A Kingdom or State may have more People in it, than the Land it contains can well support; that People therefore must be wretched, and that Government weak, till so many of the poor People, as distress each other by their Numbers, are remov'd where they can have Land to support them. The Case is the same exactly in every Nation, where the Land which is cultivated doth not afford enough to make all Things very plentiful; for this alone can make the People happy.

XII. The Quantity of Land, to be further put to Cultivation and Tillage, must be so great, as to increase the Plenty of every Thing to such a Degree, that the Price of every Thing may by that Plenty be so greatly lower'd that the Rates of Labour may

2

9 also thereby be lower'd, till Money thence come to ||
be plentiful amongst the People in general. 'Till
this End be answer'd, nothing material is effected,
nor can Trade be enlarged abroad, or relieved at
home: For the Cultivation of Land is the sole
natural Encouragement Trade can possibly receive;
because all Things must first come out of the
Ground, and, according as the Produce of the Earth
is more or less plentiful, so will the Consumption of
all Things be greater or less; that is, so much more
or less Trade will there be amongst the People. On
this the Revenue of the Nation doth so much
depend, that the whole Amount of it will be greater
or less, as this is, or is not duly encouraged; besides
that the same Sums will effect more or less accord-
ingly.

XIII. The Cash of any Nation will always decrease, and become scarce, in Proportion as the
Rents are raised, above what the Plenty of Money
circulating in Trade amongst the People, will well
enable them to pay; and where there is not Land
enough cultivated to keep down the Rents, and
thereby to remedy this Mischief, and support the
People, it may go to such an Extream, as to leave
very little Money in the Nation. For where Rents
are raised, every Thing else must and will rise too:
Whence other Nations will be able to supply our
Market; and as most of our Commodities will hence
become too dear to be taken by them in return, so
we shall vend much less of our Goods at other
foreign Markets; and so the Balance of Trade will
turn against us, and draw off our Money as long as
10 we have any. ||

XIV. Rents have been advanc'd, from this single
Principle, which alone can possibly raise the Price of
any Thing; *viz.* a Demand for Farms, &c. in greater

Proportion then they were well to be had. And as this hath in a great Measure hindered the People from going on, as such Demand for Farms shews they naturally would, in cultivating more Land as they increased in Numbers, so that Surplus or Increase of the People have been obliged to imploy themselves in Trades, Manufactures, and Professions, till they have so much overstock'd and embarras'd all these, that their Trades, &c. will not answer to support them, whilst at the same Time the Necessaries of Life, and Rents have been greatly advanc'd, to what they were formerly. This therefore must be remedied, or Multitude must be ruin'd: Nor can the Gentlemen escape; for if Money become so scarce, (as it certainly in a great Measure is at present amongst the People,) that the Fruits of the Earth will hardly bring Money enough to support the Farmers, and pay all Charges exclusive of Rent; as many Gentlemen already find, who, on that Account, are obliged to take their Farms into their own Management: The Gentlemen, I say, can fare no better than to become skilful, industrious Farmers themselves, and get their Living by that Means, till Money, as it hath heretofore been, becomes plentiful enough to pay all Charges, with a Surplus to pay Rent; which will be done whenever the Rents are lowered enough to make Money flush, or plentiful amongst the Trading Part of the People, but not sooner. || 11

XV. If all the Gentlemen in the Nation would lower their Rents, at the Request of the People, this could not answer the End; because the Demand for the Fruits of the Earth, which the Land at present cultivated can produce, is, and will continue to be so great, if the People be not diminished, as necessarily to keep the Price higher than the Money circulating amongst them will well enable them to pay for them; and because, until many more of the People are employ'd in Cultivation, &c. to lessen the Number of Poor, and make greater Plenty, all kinds of Trade, Manufactures, and Professions must needs continue so overstocked with Numbers of People imploy'd in them, as absolutely to spoil them all, as to the Profits, which is the sole End of Trade. Therefore the natural Way to lower the Rents, can only be, by putting such very great Tracts of waste Land into Cultivation, as may make Farms abound; which will lower, and make the Rents easy, and will employ the People, not in Cultivation only, but in every Kind of Manufacture, Trade and Calling. For all this will be the necessary Consequence of cultivating such large Tracts of waste Land, as must be cultivated to make Farms abound, and Rents easy.

But I am sensible, this Proposal must meet with almost an insuperable Objection, from all Gentlemen whose Estates consist of Land; since if the Plenty of every thing must be increased so much, that the Produce of the Earth may become a great deal cheaper, the Rents must be lowered a great deal too; I am so apprehensive of the Power of this Prejudice, that I fear it || will be very hard to remove it. But I shall endeavour to do it, by shewing that it is no real Loss to Gentlemen this Way to lower their Estates.

What I have said is a strong Argument to the Purpose, that the Scarcity of Money among the People will unavoidably disable the Farmers to pay their Rents. To this Cause, which doth naturally lessen the Consumption of all Things, in such Proportion as the Cash grows scarcer, and thereby keeps the Fruits of the Earth from rising to a Price, that might enable the Farmers to pay their Rents, it must be ascribed, that Corn, &c. hath hardly of late fetched Money enough to pay all Charges, exclusive of Rent; and not to the Plenty of Corn considered in itself. For cheap as Corn is, the Number of Poor, as most Parishes find, is greatly encreased of late Years; witness the Numbers we are continually transporting, and the late Invention of erecting Workhouses for the Poor, and the Complaints of Tradesmen all over the Kingdom, which have been, and are very great, and very just. Now suppose Corn, &c. were considerably advanced, to enable the Farmers to pay their Rents; what must become of the trading Part of the Nation, who already, with Justice, complain they can hardly get Money to support themselves, at the present Rates of Things? And how much more would the Poor and their Calamities increase, by such a Rise of Necessaries, together with the still greater Decay of Trade it must occasion; since if the Prices of Things were to be advanced, the People in general for want of Money must, || if possible, be still less Consumers, 13 and consequently make just so much less Business amongst them, who have already much too little? Besides, it is always found that as Trade lessens (or is divided amongst more Particulars, which is much the same Thing in Effect) the Profits of Trade lessen in still greater Proportion to the Business transacted.

But to proceed: To shew that Gentlemen will lose nothing by falling their Rents, Let it be supposed, that all the Land in the Kingdom were to be raised 20 *l. per Cent. per Annum.* Since the Land would bear no more Corn, graze no more Cattle, &c. than it now doth; must not the Corn and Cattle, &c. be considerably advanced? and must not the Labourer, whose Necessaries must then cost more, have more for his Labour? and must not Timber to make Carriages, and for every other Use, cost more to fell and hew it, &c. and must not Horses, to draw the Fruits of the Earth, &c. to Market, be more valuable; and consequently Carriage, and every Manufacture cost more too? I think all Things would certainly thus be raised, if Money could be found to circulate them at such an Advance. And then, since Gentlemen are Consumers, and must buy every thing, as well as others, at this Advance, what would they be advantaged by receiving 20 *per Cent. per Annum* more, and paying that at least, if not more, for what they want?

But if Gentlemen should say, this would be so as to what they spend; yet what they save, and lay up, would be more: For instance, suppose a Gentleman of 1000 14*l. per Annum*, now ‖ spends 500 *l.* and lays up 500 *l. per Annum*; if Estates were thus raised, he would at the same Rate spend 600 *l.* and lay up 600 *l. per Annum*: But how wou'd he be the richer, since the Price of every Thing being raised in like Proportion at least, which is an unavoidable Consequence, his 600 *l.* would purchase no more than 500 *l.* did before? Wherefore Gentlemen would, in this Case, be not one Jot advantaged. If therefore Rents should fall 30 *l. per Cent. per Annum*, every thing would certainly fall, in at least the same Proportion; so that Gentlemen would lose nothing, but the Name of so much *per Annum*; which, I think, the Argument above doth sufficiently evince. But lest the Name of losing so much *per Annum* should be a Prejudice, strong enough to prevent the Execution of this so necessary Proposal; let it be further consider'd, that empty Houses, the Number of which at present is very great, and will be greater still, if this Method be not taken to fill them; I say, empty

Houses, if they can be filled, are real Estates, as well as Land. Now if Money be thus made plentiful, as it certainly may, Plenty of Money will soon make Trade flourish, and a flourishing Trade will soon enable the People to occupy more Houses, and hereby the Number of People likewise will soon be increased *; so that Landlords taken in their || full 15 Extent, including Landlords of Houses as well as of Land, will thus certainly be Gainers, by falling their Estates so much as shall be needful to make Money plentiful; which will soon fill their Houses. But it may be said, if Lands must fall 30 *per Cent.* which is near a third, to fill the Houses; and but an eighth, or a ninth of the Number of Houses, as I shall shew, remain to be filled; how are Landlords, taken in the full Sense of the Word, including Landlords of Houses as well as of Land, Gainers? I answer, that the Rents are now raised above their proper Value; for the proper Value of any thing, is really no other, than what the Money circulating among the People will well enable them to pay; nor can any greater Value be long supported by any Means whatsoever.

But it will be asked, How we shall know when the Prices of Things are at this proper Value? I answer, that as the Price of Labour is always constituted of the Price of Necessaries, and the Price of all other Things chiefly of the Price of Labour; whenever the Price of Necessaries is such, that the labouring Man's Wages will not, suitably to his low

---

* *William Nichols*, D. D. in his *Conference with a Theist*,¹ Page 64. says, To consider farther, how mightily this Nation of ours hath increased within a Century or two; notwithstanding the many civil and external Wars, and those vast Drains of People that have been made into our Plantations since the Discovery of *America*: How the City of *London* hath doubled itself within these forty Years, notwithstanding the last great Plague; and how the Country hath increased, though not in the like, yet in a considerable Proportion, &c.

Rank and Station, as a labouring Man, support such a Family, as is often the Lot of many of them to have, the Price of Necessaries being then evidently so much too high, every thing else is so too; or then may the Prices of Things justly be said to be above this proper Value; which will more clearly appear in the Course of this Essay.

But I will proceed to shew, that the Gentlemen
16 will be the richer for falling all the Lands || in the Kingdom 20 or 30 *per Cent. per Annum*, provided this Fall be effected only by the Addition, and Cultivation of so much more Land, as will make Farms so plentiful, as to reduce the Rents of Lands so much.

For if it shall appear, that the Gentlemen would be the poorer, if all the Lands in the Kingdom were raised 20 *per Cent. per Annum*; I think the Reverse must follow, that they would be the richer if all the Lands were fallen 20 or 30 *per Cent. per Annum*; that is 70 or 80 *l.* would certainly buy more, if all the Lands were so fallen, than 120 *l.* would do, if all the Lands were so raised; which I shall endeavour to prove.

If all the Lands were raised 20 *per Cent. per Ann.* it's certain they would not produce more, but perhaps less, than they now do, by putting it, in some Degree, out of the Farmers Power to use so much Skill and Charge to cultivate them, as they could do before their Rents were so raised: I say, since the Land could however produce no more than it now doth, all the Produce, whatever it consists of, must be sold not only for all the 20 Pounds more, but there must be Profits likewise on all those 20 Pounds, to enable the Farmers to buy whatever they want at higher Prices, which every thing must needs be advanced to from thus raising the Produce,

which, as it passeth through every Hand and Manufacturing, must still have proportionably increased
Profits on the thus raised prime Cost, before it
comes to the Consumer; who, therefore, must thus
certainly, in the End, not only pay all the advanced
20 [] Pounds Rent, but likewise the necessary Profits 17
thereon through all the several Hands it must pass:
And since the Labour, which adds the greatest
Value to every thing, must in this Case be inhanced
likewise, it's evident, the same Quantity of Produce
must be dearer by all the first-advanced 20 Pounds
Rent, and by suitable Profits to all the several
Hands through which it must pass, together with a
greater Charge of Labour thereon; whence, if the
same Quantity of Produce must thus cost a great
deal more, than all the 20 Pounds Rent, by which
it was first inhanced, the Parts must cost more too
in such Proportion; so that, I think, I need not
scruple to assert, that 140 _l._ could not in this Case
purchase what 100 _l._ now doth; whence Gentlemen,
who are Consumers in common with others, would
thus evidently be much the poorer for so raising
their Estates; and therefore I think it an undeniable
Consequence, that they wou'd be the richer for
lowering their Estates 20 or 30 _l. per Cent. per Ann._
since it must be equally certain, that 70 or 80 _l._
would purchase more in this Case, than 100 _l._ now
doth; as it is certain 120 _l._ in the other Case, would
not purchase so much as 100 _l._ now doth.

And this both accounts for, and verifies an Observation, I have heard some Gentlemen make, and
wonder at, that they find they can't live so well and
hospitably on the same Estates, as their Ancestors
did, who had vastly less Income from them, than
their Successors, who make this Observation, now
have. If therefore, Gentlemen find themselves

streighten'd, by raising Rents above what the Money
18 circulat ‖ ing amongst the People will well enable
them to pay; how great must the Streights and Difficulties be which are brought on the People, out of
whom such heavy Rents are raised !

But perhaps it may be objected, that this Argument concludes too much: Since, if 70 *l.* will in this
Case purchase more than 120 *l.* why will not nothing
purchase more than something? To which I answer,
There is a proper Point, at which it will stop of
itself; which is this: Whenever the Wages of the
Labouring Man, and Price of Necessaries are made
so near equal, that he can, suitably to that low Rank
in Life, support such a Family as he, in common
with all the human Kind, chiefly came into this World
to raise, (which Things I hope to shew may be
brought much nearer together than they now are);
I say, when the Labouring Man's Wages will do this,
the Rent the Lands will then bear, is that proper
and fit Rent, which will enable the Gentlemen to
purchase more of every Thing, than any larger
Rents can enable them to do; which I prove thus:

Suppose the Rents rais'd so much, as necessarily
to carry the Price of Goods to the Consumers in
general, to higher Rates than the Money they can
get will enable them to purchase what they really
want; this makes a Kind of unnatural Plenty of
Goods, presenting themselves for Buyers, who,
though they really want them, can't find Money to
purchase them, and therefore are forced to abridge
their necessary Wants as much as they can; and this
depresses the Value of those Goods (which thus in
19 the End must want Buyers) below the Rates ‖ which
the Rents have made necessary; and this will necessarily keep the Produce of the Ground which the
Farmers bring to Market, so low, that they can't

make it answer to bear all Charges, and pay their Rents; whence the Gentlemen must find it difficult, if not impossible, to get their Rents; whilst at the same Time, whatever they buy, as hath been prov'd, will necessarily be dearer in a greater Proportion than ever the Rents can be raised; whence, I think, it must be plain, that such Rents of Lands in general, as will nearest comport with the Point above-mention'd, will always purchase most of every Thing.

But there is yet another strong Argument to induce Gentlemen to make Money plentiful; *viz.* a due Regard to the Happiness of their own Families. For let it be consider'd, that Men come into this World to raise a new Generation, and depart out of it. Now the Term of Life, Men will be found to have one with another, from the Time of Marriage to their Death, is very little more than 20 Years; in which Time, one Marriage with another, I suppose, produces about 4 Children who live to Man's Estate: Now suppose a Gentleman of 1000 *l. per Annum*, to make Provision for his Children, lays up 500 *l. per Annum*, which in 20 Years will be 10000 *l.* sav'd for them, which divided into 4 Parts, including the Widow's Share, which must often happen, can be but 2500 *l.* for each Child's Share: And since this is not only much inferior to the Estate it was sav'd out of, but hardly sufficient, *viz.* the Interest thereof, to maintain a single Person hand || somely, most of 20 the Children must be introduced into Trade, to improve their Money for their Families, or they will soon reduce it to nothing. Now if Trade be languishing and distress'd, it can't be expected but many such will sink in the general Difficulties Trade lies under. Therefore, if there be any Way practicable to make Money plentiful amongst the People in general, which never fails to make Trade flourish, it ought to be done, not only from a common Principle of Affection to the publick Good, but for the particular Benefit of every Gentleman's own immediate Offspring, many of whom are sure to be affected, just as Trade is in a flourishing or distress'd Condition.

But the languishing Condition of Trade is ascribed to the Luxury of the People; concerning which let it be consider'd,

That it is expected of every Man, that he provide for himself and Family a Support; but this Expectation is unreasonable, if Things are not so wisely constituted in their own Nature, that every one may attain this End.

The Ways Men have to attain this Support, are the Exercise of their several Occupations.

These arise solely out of the mutual Wants, &c. of Mankind. Children who can do little or nothing towards supplying themselves, make about half the Business of the World; since more than half the human Race die under 17 Years of Age.

Now if the People must retrench, they must do some or all of these Things; *viz.* wear fewer and 21 worse Cloaths, &c. eat less and worse Vic || tuals; imploy fewer or no Servants; occupy less Houseroom, and use less Light and Fewel, and spend little or no Money in any Pleasure or Diversion; and instead of Wine or strong Beer, drink small Beer or Water; and avoid Marriage, as many certainly do, because it creates a greater Expence than they can support. Now wou'd not this lessen the Consumption of every Thing, and hinder many from supporting themselves and Families, by making so much less Business amongst the People, and thereby greatly increase the Number of Poor; who, if no other Way be found to imploy them, which Tillage alone in this Case can do, must become a much greater Burthen than they are? Besides that where the Poor increase, the Profits of Trade will be still more and more reduced, through Losses. and Want of Trade, and the Efforts of such great Numbers of indigent People, as must be striving to support themselves in that Business that remains. And must not the Revenue be greatly diminish'd likewise, since in this Case the Consumption of Things, on which the Revenue intirely depends, must be lessen'd very much? Besides, 'tis certain a poor People can't pay great Taxes, any more than they can pay great Rents.

Therefore, instead of urging the People to be less Consumers, Things should be made so plentiful, that they might be greater Consumers, that Business might increase, and not abate amongst the People. And then Luxury would find its natural and proper Bounds, which if any Man transgressed in any extraordinary Measure he || would be sufficiently 22 whipt with his own Rod.

But farther; as to Luxury, those that are not influenced by the natural Motives to Frugality, will not easily be restrained by any other whatsoever.

The natural Motives to Frugality are these; present Provision for Families, and Fortunes for Children.

They who neglect the first, must soon suffer Want; and they who would provide for the latter, must consider what the Term of Life is which they may reasonably hope for, and take care that their Gains and Expences are proportioned to the End designed.

Now as Persons must, generally at least, have handsome Fortunes themselves, who shall provide

Fortunes for their Children, let it be supposed, that
a Man sets out with 2000 *l.* and by skilful and
prudent Management he gains, one Year with
another, about 500 *l.* If Men who have such Fortunes must not live a little decently, I can't see
whence Trade, which intirely depends on, and ter-
minates wholly in the Consumption of Things, can
arise; nor how Landlords can expect any considerable Rents for their Houses, *&c.* and I am certain
that to pay Rent, and Taxes, and all other Charges,
and maintain a middling Family in *London*, 250 *l.*
per Annum, is but a scanty Pattern, even where all
Things are managed with the utmost Frugality.
Nay 50 or 60 *l.* more *per Annum*, as the Rents and
the Rates of Things now go, shall hereafter be
shewn to be but a very moderate Expence.

But suppose, in this Case, such a Man should lay
23 up, one Year with another, 200 *l.* and that || for 20
Years, which is I believe much about the Term Men
have to raise and provide for Families, he then
would add 4000 *l.* to his first 2000 *l.* which makes
6000 *l.* together, to be divided amongst four Children, which I take to be the Number one Marriage
with another raises; this Sum therefore will be but
1200 *l.* for each Child's Share, if a like Sum be re-
served for the Widow; and if there should be no
Widow, but 1500 *l.* for each Child, which will not
often set them in better Circumstances than their
Parents set out in: But if Things must be worse
than this, Families must soon sink into Poverty.
And since these Things are subject to many and
great Contingencies, nobody ought to think 25 *l. per
Cent. per Annum*, even on such a Capital imployed
in Trade, too great Gain; especially considering
what Skill and Pains are necessary to reach this
End, and to what great Risk Money imployed in

Trade is always exposed, beside the present and future Provision with which Families are to be supplied out of it.

Nothing ought to be deemed Luxury in a Tradesman, whilst he lives at about half the Income of his Business; yet in Prudence he ought not to make too great a Figure, because of the uncertain and fluctuating Nature of Trade, which may happen some time or other, by Misfortune, if not otherwise, to turn against him; and because the more he can lay up for his Children, the more will he have done towards raising them to better Stations in Life.

Nor ought it to be deemed Luxury in a Tradesman if he spends the whole Income of his Business, if such Expence be unavoidable, when || the utmost 24 Frugality and good Management are exercised in such a Man's Family.

Peace and Plenty comprehend all the Felicity Mankind were designed to enjoy in this mortal State; and are so well known to constitute the Happiness of the World, that they are proverbial Terms to express the compleatest general Felicity; which undoubtedly suggests, that they have by Experience been found to answer the End.

Wherefore, if there be any Difficulty amongst the People, it must be owing to the Defect of one or both of these.

As we are now in Peace, it must be owing to the Deficiency of Plenty, that the Trade of this Nation is in such a languishing Condition; the Truth of which the numerous Complaints to the Parliament, and great Number of empty Houses abundantly evince,

Where Tillage and Cultivation of Land are not annually to a considerable Degree increased, Peace, and the natural Increase of Mankind do necessarily produce a general Decay of Trade.

For Peace, which puts an End to the vast Business which War necessarily creates, obliges those that were employed, and found their Livelihood by the Affairs of War, to employ themselves in the Business which the common Affairs of Life produce; and as hereby there is a much greater Number of People to be subsisted, on so much less Business as the ending a War puts a Period to, it's plain this must divide the remaining Business into a great many more Parts; whence the Profits, which ought to be so much augmented as the Business to each
25 Particular be || comes less (because the Expence of Living will not be less) are always found by Experience to lessen, in a greater Proportion than the Business to each Particular lessens. And this is the necessary Consequence of having a greater Number of People in any Trade, where the Business transacted by them all is no greater than when the same Trade and Business were in so much fewer Hands; and hence Ruin must happen to many whose Trades are thus unhappily circumstanced.

Besides, Peace lowering the Interest of Money brings many more People into Trade, who either cannot live on the reduced Interest of their Money, or are not satisfied to do so, and therefore enter on Trade to improve their Money to better Advantage. And such having abundance of Money to employ, must needs take a great deal of Business from those that had it before, by doing Business at much less Profit than it was before done, that they may employ the large Sums they bring into Trade; this must needs make it very difficult for People of much less Fortunes to get a Living, and of Consequence greatly increase the Number of Poor, and must needs empty the Houses too, by disabling the People to pay such Rents as they did before; and will drive many out of the Nation to get their Livings by the Arts they have learned here.

The heavy Debts and Taxes which the late War hath laid this Nation under, notwithstanding we had the greatest and most uninterrupted Success that could be wished, and have since had so long a Peace, may shew that War is not the natural Means to make Trade flourish, since the || Consequences are 26 still so burthensome to us. And if we look back to the Condition *France* was reduced to by the same War, which introduced both Famine and Pestilence amongst them, and occasioned the People to surround the *Dauphin's* Coach in Crouds, and cry out, Peace and Bread! Bread and Peace! surely these Things may fully convince us that War is a very great Calamity.

Peace, therefore, being the only natural Foundation of Happiness to any Nation, and Trade the particular Means whereby the People can be employed and subsisted, the promoting and improving Trade should be always consulted, and especially in Times of Peace, which is favourable to such a Design.

In general, there should never be any Restraints of any kind on Trade, nor any greater Taxes than are unavoidable; for if any Trade be restrained in any Degree, by Taxes or otherwise, many People, who subsisted by the Business which now hath Restraints laid upon it, will be rendered incapable of pursuing it, and of Consequence they must be employed some other Way, or drove out of the Kingdom, or maintained at the publick Charge; which last is always a great and unreasonable Burthen, and should, if there be any possible Way which might employ them, be prevented.

3

Now that there are natural Means to subsist all
Mankind in a happy Condition, will appear clear
from the Wisdom and Goodness of God, who hath
taken such ample Care of all the Creatures below
us, that they want no good thing, nor suffer any
27 Hardship but what unreasonable Men || bring upon
them. Wherefore if God hath so wisely and graciously
provided for all the Creatures below us, for whose
Happiness other Beings evidently appear to be
designed, it must be absurd to imagine he hath disposed Things so, that Unhappiness in any Degree
should unavoidably arise to Man, whom he hath
placed at the Head of all his Works in this World.
Therefore whatever Difficulties Mankind meet, must
be owing to their own Mismanagement, in not looking through the Nature of Providence with respect
to themselves.

One Branch of that Providence, which Men should
attend to and consider, is, that Mankind as certainly
increase as Vegetables, and Animals; and therefore
that Increase must continually be employed in cultivating proportionably more Land. For, otherwise
being all Consumers, there must continually be
greater Numbers subsisted on the Produce of the
same Land which was before cultivated, and this
will increase the Demand for the Produce, and inhance the Price of it, whilst the increasing People
must employ themselves solely, in Trades, Manufactures, &c. to enable them to subsist: Whence it
must needs come to pass, that Trades, Manufactures,
v; &c. will soon be so over-stocked, that all the Increase
of the People can't be subsisted this Way; seeing
the Necessaries of Life, for which they all ultimately
work, will all the while be growing dearer, and the
People less able to purchase them. And as I take
this to be very much our present Case, as may

appear by an Estimate I have subjoin'd of the necessary Expence for the Support of a poor Family, and another for || a Family in a middling Station, so this 28 Proposal of cultivating proportionably more Land, appears to me to be the only natural Remedy that can be applied; the happy Effects of which, if sufficiently executed, will soon discover it to be a universal Benefit, notwithstanding any imaginary Appearances to the contrary.

But I think it needful here to observe at what Rate Mankind increase, because their Happiness certainly depends on cultivating still more and more Land in such Proportion. And I choose to take Sir *William Pettis's*[8] Account of this, who proves Mankind will absolutely double themselves in 360 Years,* notwithstanding Wars and Plagues: Therefore, the Quantity of Land, which every Year should be taken in and cultivated, must be at least a 360th Part of the Quantity at present in Cultivation.

Now if *England* be 320 Miles long, and 290 Miles wide, it must, supposing its Length and Breadth to be every where alike, contain 92800 square Miles: But as *England* is not so regular a Figure, I suppose it will be needful to deduct a Third of its Content for its Irregularity, Towns, and Rivers; and then there will be about 62000 square Miles contain'd in it.

Now, suppose that at present, but about half, that is, 31000 square Miles are cultivated, a 360th Part of that, *viz.* 86 square Miles at least, should every Year be further added, and taken into Cultivation, to hold Proportion to the natural Increase of Mankind: And if a greater Part of *England* be already improv'd || than I have supposed, or if Mankind in- 29 crease much faster than Sir *William Pettis* above

* I take this from Dr. *Nichols.*

asserts, then the Addition every Year must be greater too in such Proportion.

But as nothing like this hath hitherto been done, it's evident to Demonstration, That hence all Trades, Occupations, Manufactures and Professions, are overstock'd with Numbers, and embarrassed. And hence Rents have been advanced by the Demand the Increase of People hath occasion'd for Land; and hence Living is become much more chargeable than formerly, and the People less able to support themselves; besides, the inhancing the Price of Necessaries hath either advanced our Commodities, or made them so much worse, that our Neighbour Nations have not taken so many of them as they would otherwise have done, and we probably must have taken more Commodities of them for this Reason. And thus, I doubt not, the Ballance of Trade is against us, that is, the Gold and Silver of this Nation have by this Means been really diminished; and the prodigious Exportation of Gold and Silver of late Years is a strong Indication of it, whatever Pretences may be advanced concerning it to the contrary. Beside that the Exchange, especially for *Holland*, hath of late Years been considerably below the Value of our Coin, as the Exchange with every Nation will always be, whenever they have the Ballance upon us *. And though this may be some small Encouragement to the Exportation of our Commodities, because they come ‖ so much cheaper to the Markets abroad, yet if our Trade goes on so, we shall certainly have very little Cash left. But if, to prevent this dreadful Evil, we do as fast as possible put a very great Quantity of Land into Use, more than at present is cultivated, our Poor

* This is a certain Rule to know when the Ballance of Trade is for or against us with any Nation.

will be employ'd, the empty Houses soon filled, and our Manufactures become much cheaper and better; and this will both increase our Exportations to the Nations we now trade with, and give Rise to other foreign Markets to vend our Goods at, and prevent the excessive Importation of foreign Goods amongst ourselves; and thus the Ballance of Trade will become in our Favour, and increase the Cash of the Nation, or Money will certainly by this Method become plentiful enough amongst the People in general. But there is no other Way in Nature to compass this End, or recover the Trade of the Nation: For those Nations that can work cheapest, must have the Money, as sure as they always will have the Trade; to which I will add, that the People will always flow into those Nations that get the Money (*i. e.* have the Ballance of Trade in their Favour) because Trade, which is the Means of getting the Money, is that which employs and subsists them.

But before I dismiss this Point, I can't help taking Notice of an Article inserted in the *Daily Courant* of *January* 3, 1731. from *Berlin*, where, it seems, an exact Register is kept of the Births, Deaths, and Marriages; by which it appears, 3332 Persons were born, and 2691 died; so that the Increase is 641 Persons that Year in that City. Now I have tried the *Par* of hu ‖ man Life from our Bills of Mortality, [31] which doth not amount to 25 Years, one with another: But, however, multiply the Deaths by 25, the Product will be 67275 Persons in that City, which divided by 641, the Increase, gives 104, the Number of Years in which Mankind will double. And if we take this for the Rule, there must be near 300 square Miles of Land more taken in and cultivated, every Year in *England*, or the Increase must fall into the several Professions, Trades, and Manufactures, and over-do, and absolutely spoil them all; which is the necessary and unavoidable Consequence of the Increase of Mankind, if Land, in proportion to the Increase be not every Year added and improved, to employ and support them.

Another Thing, which undoubtedly is of the utmost Importance to the Trade of this Kingdom, is the making Timber so plentiful, that we may build our Ships so much cheaper, that no Nation may be able to sail for less Freights than the *English*. If this be sufficiently done, together with making Labour considerably cheaper, Ships may soon be built for a Third less than they now are, which will certainly cause still many more Ships to be built here than now can be; and this will employ abundance of People of many Trades, besides the still greater Numbers who will be employed in navigating them. And as the Riches of this Kingdom do undoubtedly very much depend on maritime Affairs, so the Strength of it is chiefly its Navy: Wherefore if Timber be made very plentiful, and Labour cheaper, a Man of War may be built a vast deal cheaper too, which 32 would || make a mighty Difference in the Expence the Government are now at for the Navy, beside that they will be mann'd, and fitted to Sea at so much less Expence likewise. This will infallibly be the Consequence of sufficiently executing this Proposal in all its Parts. Thus will much less Money serve all the Affairs of the Government, and soon make a Surplus arise, to reduce the national Debts, and ease the Taxes, without any Inconvenience to the Government or the Nation.

It might be expected that Gentlemen, for their own Advantage, and the Benefit of their Families, should plant Timber enough; but we find it so much

otherwise, that Laws have been made to oblige this
to be done, and yet the End hath not been attained;
which I ascribe to these Causes: First, The Rents
having been rising of late Years, from the considerable Demand there hath been for Land, hath
been one Reason that planting Timber hath not
been sufficiently regarded. Secondly, Planting
Timber regards Posterity rather than ourselves
immediately, and this hath occasioned the Neglect
of it; and if we continue to go on thus, an Observation the *Spectator* No 583[4] recites, that the Nation
in a few Years will be at a Loss to supply itself with
Timber sufficient for the Fleets of *England*, will
certainly be verified*. Wherefore, to make Plenty
of Timber, I would propose, that a Law be made,
which shall effectually provide, and ob || lige all the 33
Lands throughout the whole Kingdom, at all times,
to maintain a Timber Tree in every Hedge and
Bank, at 100 Feet Distance or thereabouts, which
Distance I suppose sufficient to admit the Sun and
Wind, so that the Fruits of the Earth may receive
no Prejudice by the Trees that should thus grow in
the Hedges and Banks.

Further, all Lands that are infertile, or not so fit
for Cultivation; and likewise all waste Land, as far
as it's possible to effect it, should be well planted
with Timber. For it's well known that all Lands,
where Woods have been cut and grubb'd up, are
always fruitful; for a Wood, by the Fall of the
Leaves, &c. and retaining the Rain much longer on
the Ground than otherwise it would, always renders
the Ground it grows on more fruitful; besides that
Woods always produce the finest and best Timber,

---

* Timber hath been pretty reasonable these 2 or 3 Years past, which I
suppose to be entirely owing to an extraordinary Destruction of it, the
Gentlemen cutting it down in greater Quantities than usual, because the
Farmers in general have not been able to pay their Rents as formerly.

whilst the Hedges produce the strongest and crookedest; which therefore would be exceedingly useful for shipping, and especially for small Vessels. Thus Timber may be made plentiful enough, and then, if Labour be made cheaper, Ships may be built so cheap, as to enable us to cope with any Nation in the World in all maritim Affairs. But there is no other Way in Nature to do this; and till 'tis done, we must be content, not only to see the Ships of other Nations the principal Carriers of the World, but to employ many Ships ourselves which are not built in this Kingdom.

But it will be objected, This can't be effected presently, because Timber takes many Years to grow to any Perfection. So much the more Need 34 is ‖ there that it be done; and if effectual Provision be made for Futurity, the present Stock of Timber in the Kingdom will answer the End sufficiently, whilst the Supply is growing to prevent any future Inconvenience, provided Labour be, as speedily as possible, made cheap enough to contribute to that End: For the same Means which alone can make Labour cheaper, will make every other Thing cheaper. And this may be fully effected in a very few Years, and will be sensibly felt by all, from its very first Attempt, if Land enough be, as fast as may be, put into Cultivation to answer the Purpose. For with this, every Trade will infallibly flourish, without any Inconvenience but falling the Rents, which I have before shewn will be really the present Interest of every Gentleman, besides the sure Foundation of the Happiness of his immediate Off-spring.

And as to the Purchase of Estates, which is always governed by the Interest of Money, they will be valued at as many Years Purchase as they would if Rents had not fallen; and tho' the Sums they sell for must be less, in proportion as the Rents shall be lowered, yet the Money will have, at least, all the same Effects, apply it how you please.

The *Spectator* No 200,[5] asserts, That if the Fruits of the Earth could be increased one Tenth above all Possibility of Consumption, it would reduce the Price of them half. But such an Increase is absolutely impossible, the World having never yet, I believe, produced an Instance of it. Besides that the Author of the World hath, undoubtedly, observed as nice and || exact a Proportion in the Wants of Mankind, and what the Earth will produce to supply them, as he hath done in all the rest of his Works; and then such an Excess, as I said before, is impossible; and this I shall prove hereafter. ||35

But a greater Excess than this is become a Fact, as to the Houses within the Bills of Mortality*, ||36

* By the Bills of Mortality of the Year 1730, which by the preceding and succeeding Years appears to be a moderate Year, there died in *London* and *Westminster* and the Suburbs thereof,

						Years
under	2 Years old	10368	Persons; the	1 Year makes		10368
			Medium of	amongst them		
between 2	and 5	2448	which Age is	3 ½		8568
5	10	1092	13908 Under	7 ½		8190
10	20	901	10 Years.	15		13515
20	30	2048		25		51100
30	40	2471		35		86485
40	50	2373		45		106785
50	60	1713		55		94215
60	70	1577		65		102505
70	80	1601		75		75075
80	90	622		85		52870
90	100	138		95		13110
		2		101		202
		1		102		102
		2		103		206
		3		104		312
		1		105		105

By the Number of Deaths 26761, divide the Years they lived   623713, and 23 Years and about ½, according to this Bill of Mortality, appears to be the *Par* Term of human Life; multiply the Deaths by this Term, shews the Number of People living in the Bills of Mortality to be about 624,423 Persons; and if we suppose the Houses one with another to contain 10 Souls,

and will certainly be attended with that Consequence, of reducing the Rents one half, if the Method
I propose be not applied to prevent it. And if, as
he reasons in another Part of the same *Spectator*,
the Cities of *London* and *Westminster* pay a Fifth
of the whole Revenue of the Crown, beside the Rent
and Taxes they enable the Country to pay; what
Care ought to be taken to make Money plentiful
amongst the People in general, which alone can
make Trade flourish, and fill the Houses, and prevent
so great and certain a Diminution as the Revenue
must suffer in all Parts of the Kingdom for want of
this Care!

But I am sensible the great Number of empty
Houses is ascribed to the Increase of Building since
the Peace. But whoever considers, that there are
not less then 6 or 700000 People in the Bills of
Mortality; and that, according to the natural Increase
of Mankind, at the lowest Computation of doubling
in 360 Years, the Increase will be near 40000 People
37 since that Time *, he ‖will be necessarily obliged to

then the Number of Houses inhabited will be 62,442. Now the *London
Evening-Post* of *January* 2, 1732-3, says upwards of 8000 Houses, according to Account lately taken, are empty in *London*, *Westminster*, and
Places within the Bills of Mortality; most of which, let at an Average at
about 20 *l. per Annum*; at which Rate there is upwards of 160,000 *l*. Rent
yearly lost in the Bills of Mortality, more than a ninth Part of the whole
Building being empty. By this Bill of Mortality it also appears, that
more than half the human Race die under 10 Years of Age; and if we
consider the Number of young Persons, under and over this Age, who live to
supply the Places of those that die, in all the Stages of Life above this
Term, there can be no doubt that Children make about half the Business
of the World as I have asserted. And tho' it appears by this Bill of Mortality that the Term of Life, on the *Par*, is about 49 Years, excluding all
those that die at 20 Years and under, yet I can't imagine the Term Men
have to raise and provide for Families in the Marriage State doth much
exceed 20 Years, since it's pretty certain Marriages in general commence a
few Years at least later than the Age of 20 Years, and are undoubtedly
generally dissolved by the Death of one of the Parties before they both
reach the Term of 49 Years.

* I am not unsensible that Mr. *Derham* in his *Physico-Theology* shews
that the Deaths in *London* as in most great Cities are greater than the
Births, whence an Objection may seem to arise to the Increase abovementioned, which I think is of no Weight, because if a Nation will abso-

ascribe the empty Houses to other Causes, and not to the Increase of Building solely.· But however since they are built, and their being inhabited, or standing empty, will certainly have such an Influence on the Rents of the Kingdom, and the Revenue likewise, it behoves us to take the proper Methods to fill them, which I am confident will soon be effected by cultivating Land enough to make a Plenty of Money amongst the Trading Part of the People in general, but not otherwise.

But further, if the People increased, as Dr. *Nichols* says they did, so as to double themselves in *London* in 40 Years, notwithstanding the last great Plague which happened within the Period he wrote of; and the Country increased, tho' not in the like yet in a considerable Proportion (and I hope his Authority is sufficient to bear me out); then the Building since the Peace, which hath by no means I think been in proportion to one Fourth of such an Increase of People, can't be the Reason to which the vast Number of empty Houses can be ascribed.

But the empty Houses must be ascribed to such a Diminution of Trade, and consequently of Cash amongst the People, which makes it so difficult for the People to get Money to support them, that many are become incapable to pay the Rents, and many must have forsaken us on this Account. For the People will diminish, || where the Means of getting a Livelihood is not well to be attained, suitable to their several Ranks and Stations; which is a necessary Consequent, where the Balance of Trade becomes considerably against any Nation (unless the Means I contend for be taken to prevent it).

lutely double themselves in about 360 Years, notwithstanding Wars and Plagues, Cities must do so too; nay it's plain by what Dr. *Nichols* says, *London* increased at so much greater Rate as to double itself in 40 Years, notwithstanding the last great Plague which happened in that Period.

For it's evident, such a Nation hath amongst them just so much Business less than their own several Wants create, as the Amount of the Ballance against them is, which lessening their Cash at the same time just so much too, brings a double Inconvenience with it, *viz.* Want of Money and Employment: And if Things are suffered to go on so, the People must disperse and diminish. And therefore this Maxim, well known amongst Merchants, appears well founded, it being only the Reverse of what is shewn above, That the People always increase in whose Favour the Balance of Trade is considerable; as it must needs have been in ours, in that Period of Time Dr. *Nichols* wrote of; since, notwithstanding so great an Increase of the People, the Prices of every thing, as is well known, rather advanced all the Time, which they could not have done if the Cash of the Nation had not increased in yet greater Proportion than the People increased; as I think the Illustration of my fourth Maxim evinces.

Hence therefore it appears, that every Nation ought to keep Trade on such a Foot, as always, on the whole, to have the Balance in their Favour: For if Mankind double themselves only in 360 Years, if the Cash of the Nation be not augmented every Year a 360th Part, the People must in a few Years 39 be distressed for want of || Money, unless all things be made at least so much cheaper to prevent it. And as the Means of doing this is in the Power of every Nation, that have waste Land enough to improve to increase their Plenty*, and thereby reduce the Price

---

*Doctor *John Laurence*, in his *System of Agriculture*,[1] Page 45. says, Without all Question, Improvement of Lands, of what Kind soever, makes Riches and Plenty, and Plenty calls together Inhabitants, and People to consume it. And, Page 47, he says, So plain is it, that Inclosure is the greatest Encouragement to good Husbandry, and Remedy for Beggary, the Poor being imployed by the continual Labour bestowed on such Land, which is doubly repaid by the fruitful Crops it annually yields.

of Things; so the improving so much waste Land as answers this End, will furnish Employment, and consequently a Livelihood for the People; and will always, not only prevent any considerable Number of Houses from standing long empty, but will continually cause more to be added all over the Kingdom; as the vast Increase Dr. *Nichols* asserts there was, particularly in *London*, within forty Years, besides the great Increase in the Country in the same Time, doth fully shew.

But that I may put this past all doubt, let it only at present be granted, which I will shew hereafter, that the People in *London* and *Westminster* were really doubled in about 40 Years; since this, nor any thing like this, could be the Effect of the natural Increase of Mankind *, it must have some other most powerful Cause: This Cause I assert was a flourishing Trade; which I thus prove, *viz.*

The People were doubled in this Town, and ‖ in-40 creased too in the Country, though not in the like, yet in a considerable Proportion; and yet the Prices of Necessaries, and all other Things in general, were higher than those Things were 40 Years before: Now this, by my fourth Maxim, was absolutely impossible, if the Cash of the Nation had not been vastly increased also. Wherefore, as we have no Mines, the Cash could be increased only by exporting so many more Goods in value than we imported. And as this is, in itself, that which constitutes a flourishing Trade in any Nation, so we see the Effect was the doubling the People in *London* as aforesaid; wherefore let our Trade be again put on

---

* Sir *William Pettis* says, that a Nation will double their Number in 200 Years;⁸ which must always be understood thus, that it must be exempt from the Ravage of War, the Destruction of Pestilence, or being drained for distant Colonies.

such a Foot, that we may be able to raise our Produce, and Commodities of every Kind, as cheap as any Nation can raise, or make any thing whereby they may any way interfere in any Branch of our Trade, and the same Effect will again arise, and consequently not only fill the empty Houses, but cause more to be added, as I said above.

And as it hence appears absolutely needful to keep Trade on a Foot, whereby the Balance may always, on the whole, be in our Favour; so it's certain, the Mines which are continually giving Gold and Silver, do give sufficient to supply such a needful Balance to every Nation. For the Gold and Silver, which the Mines, since the *Europeans* have possess'd them, have furnished *Europe* in general with, have not only furnished Quantities equal to the Increase of Mankind since that Time, but so much more Gold and Silver, as to inhance the Price of all Kinds of Commodities in *Europe* in general, but ‖ especially in those Nations who have, either directly or indirectly, had the most considerable Trade with the Countries where the Mines are; and this in all Probability they will always continue to do; but if not, I have and shall shew how to do that which will be always equivalent.

And as to the Countries, which are thus continually furnishing this Ballance to the rest of the World, they having the Mines, have that which is equivalent to such a Balance in their Favour.

I shall now proceed to some Observations concerning Prohibitions on Trade, and also concerning prohibiting the current Coin to be exported.

It was before observed, that it is reasonably expected, every Man should, some way or other, maintain himself and Family honestly; and that, to this End, the Affairs of the World must be so wisely

constituted in their own Nature, as to furnish sufficient Employment for every Body; since any considerable Defect in this Respect must leave some
unimploy'd, and consequently without Maintenance:
And further, that there is no Employment in the
World, but what the People mutually cause each
other.

These Employments arise solely out of the several
Wants, &c. of Mankind, which constitute all the
various Trades, Professions, and Occupations of
Men; to which I will add, and hereafter prove, that
these are so wisely proportioned, as fully to employ
all that need or will be employed; and therefore
these are the natural Foundations of all Commerce
amongst Mankind || and sufficient to subsist them₄₂
all, if not obstructed by any Means.

All Nations of the World, therefore, should be
regarded as one Body of Tradesmen, exercising
their various Occupations for the mutual Benefit
and Advantage of each other.

A very considerable Part of these Employments
relate to maritime Affairs and Commerce, by transporting the Commodities of the several Nations
from one Nation to another.

This makes Ships needful, which, considering all
things that any way relate to them, furnish Employment for a prodigious Part of Mankind; besides the
inland Carriage of the Goods which the Ships are
loaded with, and the Merchants, and Writers, and
all the Trades that depend on them; which must
needs enable every Nation to support a prodigious
Number of Inhabitants, more than the same Territory could support, if there were not this Commerce
between the several Nations to employ the People.

Now since Mankind never complained of having
too much Trade, but many do really want Business

sufficient to get a Livelihood, Prohibitions do, in the
very Nature of them, cut off so much Employment
from the People, as there would be more, if there
were no such Prohibitions. And though this will, I
think, chiefly affect the Nations who prohibit the
Exportation of their own Commodities, because
other Nations will either raise those Things themselves, or substitute something else of their own, if
they can't get the same Things from other Nations,
43 which I believe one way or other they || almost always
may; yet hence 'tis evident, such Prohibitions lessen
the Number of Merchants and Ships, with all their
Appendages, so far as such Prohibitions can affect
them; which undoubtedly must cut off a Livelihood
from abundance of People, who therefore must be
obliged to seek their Livelihood in domestick Affairs;
which being not sufficient to subsist so many People,
upon the same Territory, without proportionable
maritime Trade, must bring great Inconvenience on
such a Nation, for want of so much of this Branch of
Employment for the People.

And as other Nations, for want of looking thoroughly into the Foundation of the Trade of the
World, will certainly make Reprisals by Prohibitions*, as we know they actually do, the Calamity
of every Nation, that is no wiser, will increase; since
they cut off so much Trade and Employment from
Mankind, as these mutual Prohibitions can affect.

But no Inconvenience can arise by an unrestrained
Trade, but very great Advantage; since if the Cash
of the Nation be decreased by it, which Prohibitions
are designed to prevent, those Nations that get the
Cash will certainly find every thing advance in Price,

---

* *Eras. Phillips*, Esq; in his *State of the Nation*, &c, Page 13, says
very truly, High Duties and Prohibitions on our Side beget high Duties
and Prohibitions on theirs.

as the Cash increases amongst them. And if we, who part with the Money, make our Plenty great enough to make Labour sufficiently cheap, which is always constituted of the Price of Victuals and Drink, our Manufactures, and every ‖ thing else, will 44 soon become so moderate as to turn the Balance of Trade in our Favour, and thereby fetch the Money back again. Thus Money, on which Trade floats, like a Tide, by ebbing and flowing, will bring vast Business to our People, and furnish them with Employment and Happiness. But all this doth absolutely depend on cultivating such large Tracts of Land, as will make the Plenty great enough to reduce the Price of Labour, and all other Things in consequence thereof, so as to enable us to trade on Terms as reasonable as any other Nation; without which we must shut ourselves in a great Measure out of the foreign Trade of the World; as Merchants very well know, and every body will easily believe; since they that can work cheapest, must and will have the Trade.

But those who prohibit the Exportation of the rough Principles of their Manufactures, are willing to have them exported when wrought up, and fully manufactured. Now beside that they must expect Reprisals to be made by other Nations, who will shift as much as they can without such Goods, for the sake, as they all seem to imagine, of employing their own People, not considering how much such shrinking and contracting their Trade within themselves, cuts off the more valuable maritime Trade and Employment, which all should strive to promote and enlarge, not only for the Reason I gave before, but because such Nations will always be the richest and most powerful (in respect to the Bigness of their Territory) who have the most maritime Trade,

4

whether the Quantity of Cash amongst the People be as great as any other Nation or not; beside all 45 this, I ‖ say, it may not be amiss to consider, what a vast Value must be risqued at Sea, when Things are fully manufactured, to what would be risqued in their rough Principles; and what a Tendency the vast Value of Goods, fully manufactured, hath to make the Balance of Trade fluctuate, so as to hazard very great Quantities of Gold and Silver, much oftener at Sea, to make the Balance, than there otherwise would be Occasion for: And after all, how difficult is it, sufficiently to prevent the Exportation or Importation of any thing, which those who want it will be at the Charge to get; and what a Damage do a great many honest People sustain, by the un-avoidable Inconveniencies attending Prohibitions and high Duties, besides the Iniquity they too often occasion! But let us a little consider, whether a free and unrestrained Trade hath any Inconveniencies, we ought to guard against *. I will not contend for it, with respect to *France*, though I can't see it could do us any Harm, even in that Case, if we were prudent enough to prevent the Inconvenience, by employing more Land as our Cash decreases, there-by to employ the People, and lower the Price of Things still so much, that whatever Cash remains amongst us, it may however be so plentiful as to circulate Trade to the utmost, and so make the People in general happy, notwithstanding its De-crease. For I am sensible that as *France* can work 46 vastly cheaper, because ‖ they can live for a great deal less than we can do, so they can make most of

---

* *Eras. Phillips*, Esq; Page 14. gloriously says, A trading Nation should be an open Ware house, where the Merchant may buy what he pleases, or sell what he can. Whatever is brought to you, if you don't want it, you won't purchase it; if you do want it, the Largeness of the Impost don't keep it from you.

the Manufactures we make, as well as we can; and therefore if we were to open Trade with them, they would bring us all sorts of Goods so cheap, that our Manufactures would be at an End, till the Money they would by this Means get of us rais'd the Prices of their Things so much, and our Want of Money should fall ours to such a Degree, that we could go on with our Manufactures as cheap as they; and then Trade would stand between that Nation and us, as it doth between us and other Nations who mutually take Goods of each other; and I think this would enlarge the maritime Trade of both Nations, together with all the Trades relating thereto (*i. e.* would furnish still further Means of employing abundance of People of both Nations this Way); and at last, this will terminate in the particular Advantages each Nation naturally hath in the Produce of their respective Countries: And if any Nation is blest in this respect more than another, the Difference this will make, will be only that of having more Money amongst them, than such other Nations have in proportion to the Number of their People, and the Prices of Things in each Nation will be dearer and cheaper respectively; yet if they should go to make any other Advantage of this, to restrain, and so increase the Money amongst them, this would soon prove to their Hurt, because as their Goods will certainly rise as their Cash increases, so this will make the Opportunity greater for other Nations, who will from hence be able to outdo them in Cheapness, to drive them out of || their Trade at other 47 foreign Markets, and probably, notwithstanding all they can do to prevent it, such cheap Commodities will find the Way to them likewise.

But we must consider our Trade, with respect to all other Nations, as well as *France*. Suppose, therefore, that such an unrestrained Trade with *France*, or any other Nation, should diminish our Cash so very considerably, that we could not give above half the Price for Things in general as we at present do: if we take care to keep our Trade alive, by employing the People in cultivating more Lands, that our Produce and Manufactures may be cheap enough to carry on Trade with such Nations, it must needs enlarge our Trade mightily with those Nations, whose Cash keeps their Prices of Things near to, or above the Rates ours are now at; insomuch that I think we must needs have the Balance on all such Nations, so much as to prevent any considerable Mischief arising to us, whilst our Trade is taking such a Turn as an open Trade with those Nations, who can work so much cheaper, might occasion.

But lest any should think my laying such Stress on cultivating so much Land is any way extravagant, I would desire them to consider, that this also will find its natural Bounds; for the cultivating Land will stop of itself, when the Plenty becomes too great to answer and turn to Account; which can only arise from too high Rents, or employing too many of the People this Way; of which last I apprehend there never can be any Danger, as I will shew hereafter. But if this could be, since the People make
48 a || Shift to live now, there is an evident Necessity to cultivate a great deal more Land to employ them, and thereby to make Money plentiful, and Trade to flourish. How profitable and advantageous would all other Trades, *&c.* become, by being thus in fewer Hands than they would require*; to which the great Plenty and Cheapness of Necessaries, which is ultimately what all work for, would so mightily contri-

---

* This will in the Course of this Essay appear to be a necessary Consequence in this Case.

bute, that the People would naturally fall into them, and so hold that Proportion in all Trades, Manufactures, and Professions, as well as Cultivation of Land, that the Nature of Things themselves would plainly and sufficiently point out! And the Rise of Rents of late Years, which like all other Things could only rise from the extraordinary Demand for Lands, is a Demonstration that all Things would certainly thus work of themselves, just as they should do, and as the Author of Nature designed, if the People could have had more Land, instead of raising the Rents, as they wanted it; for this is really that Course of Providence, which is established in the Nature of Things, for the Provision and Happiness of Mankind.

I shall now proceed to shew that the prohibiting the current Coin to be exported is certain Loss to the Nation. For we can have no Occasion to send Money, or Bullion, or foreign Coin to any Nation, unless we receive more Goods in Value from them than they have from us; in which Case they must have our Money or Bullion, or foreign Coin, sent them, or we must cease to trade || with them, which 49 I think is impossible. Now if I must buy Bullion or foreign Coin, because the Exportation of our Coin is prohibited, it's certain that the Seller of Bullion or foreign Coin must and will have a Profit; that is, I must give more in Coin for less in Bullion or foreign Coin, which when my Correspondent receives, he will value it just as if it were our own Coin of like Weight and Fineness: Wherefore if the Demand continues here for Bullion or foreign Coin, to pay the Balance of Trade to any Nation, he will send it back to this Market, where it must and will in this Case fetch more, by all Charges of Freight, and Risque of the Sea, and Postage of Letters, and

Commission, and some Profit to himself; unless our Coin be melted to save this Loss. Now suppose all this should make but 2 *per Cent*. it's evident that in 50 Returns of the Bullion of foreign Coin, we must have paid a whole Capital more than if we were admitted freely to send our own current Money, where the Balance of Trade requires it. And this must cause our current Money to be melted both at home and abroad, since it will thus be worth 2 *per Cent* more than it is in Coin; and the more the Ballance of Trade lies against us with any particular Nation, so much the quicker will these disadvantageous Returns be made, and our Specie undoubtedly be so much the faster melted. But if we let our current Coin come and go freely, Bullion or foreign Coin will not be worth so much as our Coin, because its Fineness and Value cannot be so easily and universally known; and therefore if the Balance of Trade 50 be in our || Favour, that is, brings us Gold and Silver, it must and will go to the Mint to be coined, to ascertain its Fineness and Value, provided the Government not only coin it at their own Charge, but immediately deliver as many Ounces of Coin as they receive of foreign Gold and Silver; for it's no less absurd for the Government to fix the Price they will give for Gold and Silver brought to be coined, than it would be to make a Law to fix and ascertain the Prices of every other Commodity.

And it's further certain, that as the Balance of Trade is a fluctuating Thing, if our Money be suffered to go and come freely as the Balance of Trade may require, (and otherwise it neither can go nor come) as Bullion will then certainly be of somewhat less Value than Coin, the People in foreign Nations will buy up what Money of ours they can easily find, because it will hardly be of so much Value amongst

them as their own, and they can pay more with it in
the Nation it properly belongs to than with Bullion
or their own Coin; and this will certainly in a great
Measure prevent the melting our Money at home,
and in foreign Nations, and consequently will save
the Trouble and Charge of coining a great deal of
Money, and bring a great deal of our Money back
from those Nations where the Balance of Trade had
before carried it, provided our Trade stands on
such a Foot with those Nations, that the Balance be
in our Favour: And I have shewn how it may certainly be made so, *viz.* by making our Produce and
Manufactures so plentiful, and thereby (which is inseparable) so cheap and good, as to cause ‖ foreign 51
Nations to take abundance more of them; which
Plenty and Cheapness of our Produce and Manufactures will prevent the Importation of abundance
of foreign Commodities; and thus the Balance will
be in our Favour, and that Balance must be paid us
in Money: By this Means only it is we have any
Gold and Silver, *i. e.* Money amongst us; nor is there
any other in Nature, for any Nation that hath not
Mines: Wherefore this deserves the utmost Regard
of every Trading Nation, not only for the Sake of
the Money they will thus get, but to make their
Trade flourish, and their People happy, and their
Government powerful; for without this, Trade must
languish, the People become poor, which will make
the Taxes an insupportable Burthen, and consequently make the Government weak.

I think this the more concerns us, because Foreigners are interested in our publick Securities and
Funds for vast Sums; for, low as we think the Interest of Money to be now, we give better Interest
than they can make at home; and our Parliamentary
Securities having been always maintained inviolably,

give every body the utmost Confidence in them. As therefore all Commodities (and Money is no other) ever did, and ever will find the highest Market, so this is the Cause why Foreigners deposit their Money in our Funds; and as they thereby draw home the Interest, they contribute so much to the decreasing the Cash of the Nation.

Another thing, which still enforceth the Argument to permit our current Coin to go and come freely, 52 as the Balance of Trade may re ‖ quire, is, that if we have the Balance of Trade in our Favour, on any Nation who hath the Balance in their Favour on another which hath the Ballance on us, such Nations will probably transmit our Money to the Nation that has the Balance on them; because if they send their own current Coin, it will be as much foreign Coin to the Nation it's sent to, as our Coin can be; and therefore, as I said, if we have the Balance on any Nation which receives our Money, it will come back again to us, because it will pay more and be readier, than if they sent us Bullion or their own current Specie; and thus will it save our Money from being melted abroad as well as at home; which I think a strengthening Argument for permiting our Specie to go and come freely where the Balance of Trade shall carry it.

In the Beginning of this Essay, it was laid down as a Maxim, That Gold and Silver (*i. e.* Money) will be plentiest where the Mines are: Now since I am treating of prohibiting our current Coin to be exported, let it be supposed, that the People possess'd of the Mines could furnish themselves with the Necessaries and Pleasures of Life by the Produce of their own Country, and therefore should think fit to prohibit the Exportation of Gold and Silver, and should thereby be effectually able to prevent the Exportation thereof; which is undoubtedly impos-

sible: I say, if we suppose such Nations to prohibit
the Exportation of Gold and Silver, and at the same
time continue to work those Mines, so that they are
continually giving more and more Gold and Silver,
how great must the || Increase of those Commodities 53
soon become! And since Gold and Silver are of
little Use, besides procuring the Necessaries and
Conveniencies of Life, which alone are real Riches,
and for which Gold and Silver are now universally
exchanged; would not the great Plenty of these
Commodities, thus continually increasing, cause
proportionably so much more Gold and Silver (with
which they would at length be incumbered) to be
given for the more necessary Produce and Fruits
of the Earth? And would not this so depress the
Value of Gold and Silver, by their Plenty amongst
them, as to give ample Opportunity and Encouragement to all theWorld to go to this Market with their
Produce and Manufactures, which they can and will
sell for a vast deal less Gold and Silver, than what
such Goods of their own raising would in this Case
be sold for? Nay, they would find it a Convenience
to be eased of the Burthen of Gold and Silver, which
the Mines, if continually worked, would be giving,
as certainly as it's a Relief to any Country to part
with any Commodity they too much abound in: For
if they do not cease to work the Mines, when they
have raised Gold and Silver enough to be burthen-
some, they must and will certainly drop their Cultivation and Manufactures; since Men will not easily
be induced to labour and toil, for what they can get
with much less Trouble, by exchanging some of the
Excess of their Gold and Silver for what they want.
And if they should be supposed, as is natural enough
in this Case, to drop their Cultivation and Manu-
factures, which are much the slowest and most la- || 54

borious Way of supplying themselves with what they could so easily and readily procure by exchanging Gold and Silver, which they too much abound in, they would certainly, in a great Measure, by so doing lose the Arts of Cultivation, and especially of Manufactures; as it's thought *Spain* hath done, merely by the Accession of the Wealth which the *West-Indies* have produced them; whence they are become a poor Nation, and the Conduit-Pipes to disperse the Gold and Silver over the World, which other Nations, by making Goods cheaper than they can do, are fetching from them, to such a Degree, as that the Mines are scarcely sufficient to answer their Occasions; and though they are sensible of this, yet they find by Experience they can't prevent it.

The Case is the very same, in some Degree, in every Nation, whose Quantity of real or artificial Cash is large enough to support the Prices of their Goods, considerably above the Rates such Goods bear in other Nations round about them. Whence it's obvious, all Prohibitions must in the Issue be injurious to Trade, because beside all other Mischiefs they occasion, they are always designed to restrain the Money from going out of the Nation.

Yet I must own, I am entirely for preventing the Importation of all foreign Commodities, as much as possible; but not by Acts of Parliament, which never can do any good to Trade; but by raising such Goods ourselves, so cheap as to make it impossible for other Nations to find their Account in bringing them to us: And as this is the only natural and
55 effectual Prohibition of || such Things as we would not receive from abroad, so I wish every Nation in the World would do this as much as ever they can; for then the Plenty of every thing would be so great, that all Mankind would be happy, if this World is capable of making them so.

I shall now proceed to some Observations upon the whole.

First, That it is of no Consequence, whether any Nation hath a vast deal of Gold and Silver, or but very little Money amongst them, if sufficient Care be taken to make the Plenty of every thing great enough, to make the Money they have, amply extend to circulate their Trade in every Branch, so as fully to employ and support all their People; which must and will make them all happy, and certainly cause them to have vastly more foreign Trade, by their thus being able to make and sell their Manufactures and Produce at lower Rates than their Neighbour Nations can do. And this is absolutely in the Power of every Nation, that will cultivate Land enough to effect it; unless any Nation should have more People in it than they have Land to support them; which may easily be known from the Demand there will be for Land, and raising the Rents in Consequence thereof, till the Prices of Necessaries become so dear, that the Wages of the labouring People will not purchase what is needful for the Support of their Families, and there be no more Land left to cultivate, and remove this Mischief, which will fall more or less on every Occupation, in Proportion as the Poor become thereby distressed. In this Case, there is no Relief but transporting the People where they can have Land enough for them.|| 56

Secondly, It's of little or no Consequence to the Trade of any Nation, whether the People spend near or all their Gains, provided they do not spend more than they really gain; for this disables them to make good their mutual Contracts and Bargains; or whether they are generally frugal, and lay up considerably. For the Trade of a Nation doth very little depend on these Things, but intirely on employing

the People in Cultivation of Land, in that Proportion
to the other Employments of Mankind, that the
Necessaries of Life, which all ultimately work for,
may be so plentiful, that the meanest of the People
may easily attain a Sufficiency of them; for Plenty
of these comprehends all human Felicity, not ex-
cepting Peace itself. For why should we differ, or
go to War; or how can we ask Heaven to succeed
our Arms against our Neighbours, when we have
enough of what we want amongst ourselves, and
can sell our Produce, and make our Goods so cheap,
as almost to lay them under a Necessity to buy
them of us? And this is the best Condition our
Trade with foreign Nations can ever have, and will
render all other Stipulations and Treaties about our
Trade, almost, if not altogether unnecessary. So
that we may very well maintain Peace with all the
World, if they do not mediately or immediately
attack or make Depredations upon us; in which Case
alone I apprehend it can be justifiable to suffer so
many People to be cut off, as War necessarily de-
stroys on both Sides. And if every Nation would
pursue these Things, each would be so far from in-
juring another, that every one would contribute to
₆₅ the Happiness of the whole. ||

And since I have asserted the Connection of
Plenty and Peace to be such, that they may always
be maintained together, and support each other, I
shall shew how to avoid a War, in all Cases, except
that of one Nation's making Depredations on the
Goods or Territories of another; in which Case, the
Aggressors so kindling War are the greatest
Plagues and Murderers of Mankind, with whose
Calamities they are justly chargeable.

I would by no Means have any Nation tamely, or
easily give up the minutest Advantage in Trade

they justly possess; and whoever will force such Advantages from them, invades their just Rights and Properties, and may therefore undoubtedly be repell'd by Force of Arms.

Yet we should not easily be drawn into a War, it being one of the greatest Calamities to which Mankind can be subjected; the End of which none can well foresee, and the Burthens of which (*i. e.* publick Debts and Taxes) are seldom discharged in one Generation, tho' a Peace of so long Duration should happen to ensue; not to insist on the prodigious Devastations War often makes, and the tributary State Nations are sometimes brought under by it: On this Account, I say, we should not easily be drawn into a War, but rather give up an important Point of Trade, if it can't be preserved without a War, the Success and Duration of which we find ourselves not able to determine when we engage in it.

For why do Nations contend about Points of Trade? Is it not solely for the Sake of the Money they shall get by it? || 66

Now if this be a true Principle, that the Price of the Produce and Manufactures of every Nation will advance, as the Cash amongst the People increaseth; if we, to avoid a War, prudently give up a Point of Trade which augmented our Money, we must then for want of such Point of Trade, and that Money, make every thing so much cheaper at home, by the Means I have shewn, as that we may be able to go with our Produce and Manufactures, still so much cheaper than before, to those Nations whose Markets will now be considerably advanced by the Money they get by the Points of Trade we parted with to them. Now if our Produce, *&c.* be made cheap enough, as I have shewn they certainly may they will force themselves on them, and find so much

more Vend at such Markets, as to supply them even
with what before they either raised themselves, or
had from other Nations, and at the same time
prevent them from sending many of their Goods to
our Markets, where all Things being thus made
plenty, and consequently good, will be too cheap to
admit the much dearer Commodities of other Nations. And thus we may have the Balance on any
⌐such Nation, and bring home the Money thro' their
Canal, even though we give up such considerable
⌐ Points of Trade, by which they first get the Money
⌊we should otherwise have had.

And if there really be this Way, as there undoubtedly is, for every Nation, that will be so prudent
sufficiently to pursue it, to preserve Peace, and extend their Trade, and avoid War; how absurd as
67 well as wicked is it to go to War ‖ about Trade,
which we hence see may be more effectually promoted by the Arts of Peace! And this I think is a
wise Disposition of Providence, shewing how Mankind may maintain Commerce and Peace over the
Face of the whole Earth, without interrupting the
one, or breaking the other.

Thirdly, The full and sufficient Execution of this
Proposal, is the only natural Means to prevent the
clandestine Exportation of our Wool; for it's evident,
since there are the best Laws and severest Penalties,
that could well be devised, already made to prevent
the running our Wool, whoever will have it must
wade through all the Difficulties and Impediments
that lie in their Way; which can't possibly be done
without very great Charges, and sometimes losing
the Wool they are endeavouring to run; whence our
Wool must needs come vastly dearer to those Nations that so fetch it from us, than what the same
Wool costs our own Manufacturers; wherefore, if the
People in foreign Nations could not live a vast deal

cheaper than we can do, they could not be able to work so much cheaper, as to prevent us from sending them our Manufactures. But because the Necessaries of Life cost them a vast deal less than those Things cost us, therefore notwithstanding our Wool costs them a vast deal more, for the Reasons above assigned, than it cost us, yet they are able by this Means to make the Manufactures cheaper for themselves than they can have them from us *; and this

---

* Mr. *Benjamin Ward* of *Yarmouth*, in his State of the Woollen Manufactory considered,[10] who seems to have informed himself thoroughly of this important Branch in foreign Nations, says, Page 4. "It's certain no
' Country in *Europe* manufactures all Kinds of Goods so dear as the People
' of this Kingdom, which gives other Nations a vast Advantage in carry-
' ing their Manufactures to Market, and enabling them to become our
' Rivals in Trade to almost all Countries; and a little lower he says, 10
' Pound and a half of Wool from the Sheeps Back will make a Piece of
' Calimanco weighing eight Pound, which Wool will cost our Manu-

	l.	*s.*	*d.*
' facturers			
' about	0	6	0
' the manufacturing thereof will cost	1	4	0
' So that the Piece will cost us	1	10	0
' But though Foreigners must be at so great a Charge			
' to get our Wool, that the same Quantity will cost them			
' double, that is,	0	12	0
' yet being able to manufacture the same for	0	12	0
which is	1	4	0

' they can and do undersel us 6 Shillings, which is 20 *per Cent* in such a
' Piece, of which he says, the manufacturing Part is as little as any Stuff
' we make; wherefore, as he says, Page 9. we are under an absolute Neces-
' sity to make our Goods as cheap as possibly we can, if we mean not to
' lose our foreign Trade''.
    And I say there is no way to do it but to reduce the Necessaries of Life to half their present Price, that we may work as cheap as any Nation that now interferes in any of our Manufactures or Branches of our Trade, which may certainly be done the Way I propose; and this will infallibly remedy all the Evils the foreign or domestick Trade of this Kingdom any ways suffers, and will make Money sufficiently plentiful amongst all Ranks of People, together with it; for these Things shew themselves, or are self evident.
    Eras. Phillips, Esq; Page 8. says, 'Next to lessening the Price of
' Labour is to bring down the Price of Wool: It hath been in a great
' Measure owing to the Dearness of our Woollen Manufactures, that both
' *Holland* and *France* have thought it worth their Care to set up Looms of
' their own, to our great if not irreparable Detriment; and *France* hath so far
' succeeded, that she seems to have no further Occasion for our Cloaths at all.
    ' And *Holland* hath found out this Secret of Trade to buy up our Raw
' Cloaths, if I may be allowed the Expression, and dye and nap them so
' much cheaper than we, that they are able to undersel us in Goods of our
' own Produce.

68 is both the || Cause and Encouragement of the running our Wool, and enables those that so fetch it from us, to interfere with us, at other foreign Markets, with the Manufactures they make of our Wool, since they can make them cheaper than we 69 can, and, for ought I can see, they might be || able, if they could get these Manufactures imported amongst us, to beat us out of this Branch of our Trade even amongst ourselves, if we should continue to keep the Necessaries of Life so dear as to prevent our Manufacturers from working cheaper.

But if we make our Victuals and Drink so much cheaper, as shall enable us to work as cheap as other Nations can do*, the running our Wool will stop of itself; for we shall then be able to send them our Manufactures so cheap, as to prevent them from putting themselves to such extraordinary Difficulties and Charges to get our Wool, as they now certainly must do if they will have it from us.

And as this is the natural Means to prevent the running our Wool, so, I believe, I may be positive the Woollen Manufactures in *England* will never be promoted or relieved any other Way whatsoever; because whilst the Necessaries of Life cost so much as they now do amongst us, most other Nations will be able to work a great deal cheaper than we†. And

---

* This must not be done by making the Poor fare harder, or consume less than their reasonable Wants in that Station require; for they being the Bulk of Mankind would in this Case affect the Consumption of Things in general so mightily, that there would be a Want of Trade and Business amongst the other Part of the People, which will affect the Rents so much the more as the People this Way shall be distressed; but this must be done by imploying the Poor the right Way (*i. e.*) in Tillage and Cultivation of Land, to make the Plenty so great that they may have their Wants properly supplied for that Station of Life, and yet work so cheap as to make our Produce and Manufactures as cheap, as any of our neighbouring Nations make any thing whatsoever, wherewith they any Way interfere in any Branch of our Trade.

† 'Tis a wrong Notion, that if our Poor who take Alms, were obliged to work at our Manufactures, instead of being assisted, that our Manufac-

if thereby ‖ they are really found able to interfere in 70 almost the only natural Branch of our Trade, how much more must this affect us in many other Branches of our foreign Trade, beside the Encouragement they by this Means find to vend their Wares to us, whilst our Commodities are by this Means too dear to find sufficient Encouragement at any of those foreign Markets that can work cheaper than we?

But to encourage our Woollen Manufactures, we ought most certainly to make them cheaper, that many of our own People, who now go in Rags, and almost naked, may be able much easier to purchase Cloaths; and many others may be more frequently cloathed than they are, or, I believe, as Things now stand, they can be; but as this can't be done but by employing abundance more of our People in Cultivation of Land, so the employing them this Way, which will certainly make Things cheaper to what Degree we please, will also enable the People to purchase such Cloaths as will defend them from the Cold and Weather, and put it in the Power of abundance of People to be sweet and clean, who are now, without Remedy, a Reproach not only to our Country, but even to human Nature itself.

And thus I think our Woollen Manufactures, which now even lie by and spoil, or rot in our Warehouses, would be certainly wanted, and used as fast as they could be made by our Manufac ‖ turers; and this, I 71 think, would save our Government the Charge they are now at for Officers and Vessels to prevent the running our Wool, which I suppose can't be an inconsiderable Article.

tures would thence become cheaper; the Poor wou'd in this Case soon make Labour so little worth as to starve each other, and then they must forsake that Business, be it what it will; and then those Manufactures must again fetch a Price that will pay all Charges, and support the Labourer, or they must cease to be made.

5

For such a greater Consumption of our Wool at home would take up a good Part of that Surplus, which perhaps, as things now stand, would make Wool of little Value, if Foreigners did not fetch it clandestinely from us; and what a Tendency this hath to make our Gentry connive at the running our Wool, to enable the Grower to pay his Rent, I shall leave to every one's own Reflection.

Fourthly, The full and sufficient Execution of this Proposal will lessen the Number of Hawkers and Pedlars, and all other Tradesmen in every Business, which is now overstocked with Numbers, by making it more profitable to them to employ themselves in transacting the Trade and Affairs, that must necessarily arise by increasing the Produce of the Earth to so very considerable a Degree, as will be needful to attain the End I am persuing in this Essay.

For if so great a Quantity of waste Land were annually added and cultivated, as would hold Proportion not only to the natural Increase of Mankind, which I have shewn must at present be at least 86 square Miles every Year; and if so much more waste Land were also added, as would lower the Price of Necessaries so much as shall be effectual to enable the Poor to work considerably cheaper, than they now can do; as there then would be a prodigious deal of Work created, which is now wanted to em-
72 ploy || the Poor, and enable them to subsist without being chargeable to the Publick, that they, together with many others, may become much greater Consumers, than ever they can be, till the Plenty of every thing is rendered great enough to admit so much greater Consumption; so this would certainly make abundance of Trade and Business for Shopkeepers and other Venders not only of this extraordinary Quantity of Produce, but of all kinds of

Manufactures, which will most certainly be made and consumed at home, or vended abroad, in consequence of the Plenty of these Things arising from the continual Addition of so much waste Land every Year: I say therefore, as this must needs create a prodigious deal of Trade for Venders of all sorts of Goods, more than now exists, or can exist till this be done, so it must needs cause many of those, who now, to get their Bread, travel the Country with Packs and Burthens enough to break their Backs, sometimes Miles before they come to an House, where after they have taken so much Pains they often sell nothing; I say, this must needs cause many such Hawkers and Pedlars to employ themselves at their own Habitations or proper neighbouring Markets, and prevent others, by making it unnecessary, and not so well worth while, from entering on so laborious and painful an Employment as Hawkers and Pedlers do and must submit to; besides that to save the extraordinary Charges which are almost unavoidable to Travellers, they not only fare hard, but commonly lodge in Barns.

Wherefore if this Proposal were to be executed, the Number of Hawkers and Pedlars would || cer- 65 tainly be so much lessened that they would be no such Injury to Shop-keepers as their almost universal petitioning against them to the Parliament, and the very Nature of hawking Goods about Town and Country shews they certainly are, and must continue to be, not only to Shop-keepers, but to Landlords of Houses too, because they disable the Shop-keepers to pay the Rents.

And as this Proposal is the only natural Means to lessen the Number of Hawkers and Pedlars, and all other Tradesmen whose Trades are too numerous, so I believe it's the only possible Way to remove

the Mischief now brought on most Trades by hawking Goods; for in almost every Trade, even where
vast Sums are employed, and where they can't carry
their Goods from place to place, it is become a Rule
to court and solicit Customers in Town and Country,
not only to the great and unreasonable Reduction
of the Profits of Trade, which when hawking Goods
thus becomes general, will be inseparable to this
Practice, but also to the very great and extraordinary
Expence of every Tradesman, who will put in for a
Share of Trade, and not stay at home whilst others
pick away his Customers; besides that the Customers
so obtained are often in such Circumstances, as
occasion the making more and larger bad Debts,
than would probably be made if Goods were not
pushed off by such extraordinary Means; but if what
I here propose be executed, all these Evils will be
so far remedied, that it will be every Man's chief
Interest to keep his Shop, because his Shop will
66 then keep him. ||

Fifthly, The full and sufficient Execution of this
Proposal, will in a great Measure prevent the giving
long Credit, and making bad Debts in Trade.

For long Credit increases the Sums credited,
because People in longer Time wanting still more
and more Goods, makes the Sums credited much
larger than they would be, if Credit were considerably shortened in point of Time. Wherefore such
long and large Credit, doth very much contribute
to the making bad Debts, which, I think, is not only
obvious but sadly felt too, by a great many; if therefore the executing this Proposal, will in some good
Degree prevent the giving long Credit, it must also
in a great Measure prevent making bad Debts.

Now the giving long and large Credit, is undoubtedly owing only to such Trades being too

numerous, whence the People in such Trades, in order to vend their Goods, find themselves under a Necessity, if they will get any thing by them, to trust large Sums a long Time. But if the Way I contend for, of furnishing Tradesmen with more Business, were put into Practice, the giving long and large Credit would generally cease; for as in this Case, there would certainly be larger Business in fewer Hands, this would (and nothing else can) enable Tradesmen to pick and choose whom they will credit, whereas they now certainly are forced to court and oblige almost any body that will take their Goods, where they have any tolerable Prospect to have the Money for them, with what Credit and Time such Customers please to take; whence not only very slow Returns of Money are made, || but great Losses 67 and Ruin befalls many Tradesmen who had pretty good Beginnings, and who, if their Trades had not been thus unhappily circumstanced, would probably have made considerable Improvements.

Besides, the doing what I contend for, would certainly mend the Circumstances of the People in general very much, which would render long Credit the less necessary, and make the Risk of bad Debts inconsiderable to what it is, where the People in general are in such strait and bad Circumstances, as to stand in need of long and large Credit. And thus also would much less Sums employed in Trade, be sufficient for much larger Transactions or Returns, than when long and large Credit is become the Course of any Trade, which will always unavoidably be the State of every Trade that is overstocked with Numbers.

But it may be said, that the giving long Credit, is rather owing to the Plenty of the Commodities credited, than to the Number of Traders in such Commodities.

But since the Plenty of such Commodities is owing
to employing too many Hands in raising them, in
which Case, there will always be too many to vend
them, long Credit is still owing to such Trades being
too numerous, and overdone in all the several Parts.

But the Plenty of the more immediate Necessaries
of Life, can, I think, never be overdone, because the
cheaper these are, which is inseparable from the
Plenty of them, the greater will the Consumption of
them be, since they will hence be more easily attained
68 in much larger ‖ Quantities by almost all Ranks of
Men; and as these are what all Men chiefly and
ultimately work for, in whatever Way they are employed, so they are the principal and proper Foundation of the Plenty and Cheapness, and consequently of the proper Consumption of all other
Things whatsoever. For to what Purpose is it to
abound in all kinds of Manufactures, if the People
are generally scarce able to procure themselves the
other more immediate Necessaries of Life, Victuals
and Drink?

But though the Rents must be lowered, as these
Things shall, by the Plenty of them, be made cheaper,
yet having before shewn that all Things will hence
become cheaper, in much greater Proportion, than
the Rents will be lowered, I shall only say further,
that since all Things must first come out of the
Ground, Lands will always bear such Rents as the
Cash circulating amongst the People, consistently
with the general Welfare, will naturally support;
and higher Rents they never can bear, without
greatly distressing the People in general, and the
Gentlemen themselves too in the End, of which the
Multitude of Farms, which have of late been quitted
through the Inability of the Farmers to pay the
Rents, are a sufficient and melancholy Proof. For

the Rents of Lands are undoubtedly as much subjected to the Quantity of Cash circulating amongst
the People, as it has been clearly shewn the Price
of Goods necessarily is.

And hence I conclude, that it is owing to too great
a Scarcity of Money amongst the People in general,
which doth necessarily lessen the Consumption of
every thing so much, that the || Price of the Produce 69
of the Ground can't be raised high enough to enable
the Farmers to pay all Charges, and live and pay
such Rents as they were to have paid.

Sixthly, The full and sufficient Execution of this
Proposal, would be a vast Encouragement to young
People to marry; since the Means of a Livelihood
for Families, would hereby be vastly facilitated, and
hereby the Marriage State would be relieved from
the melancholy Difficulties it now too generally lies
under, for want of striking out greater Plenty, and
more Employment, to enable those that are in it, to
support and make Provision for their Families, suitably to their several Ranks and Stations.

And those unjust Reflections, too frequently cast
on the Marriage State, would cease with those Difficulties, which is the general Foundation of them all;
and we should sing with *Milton*, Book 4th,

Hail wedded Love, mysterious Law, true Source
Of human Offspring!
By thee adulterous Lust was driven from Men,
Amongst the bestial Herd to range; by thee,
Founded in Reason, loyal, just and pure,
Relations dear, and all the Charities
Of Father, Son, and Brother, first were known.
Here Love his Golden Shafts employs, here lights
His constant Lamp, and waves his purple Wings;
Reigns here, and revels; not in the bought Smile
Of Harlots, loveless, joyless, unindear'd.

The full and sufficient Execution of this Proposal 70 would cause much less Fortunes to be re || quired with young Women; since not only much less Sums would transact much larger Affairs, but there would abundance more Business every way arise to be transacted; whence the young Men would not have Occasion for such Precautions, as are now absolutely needful to all that will marry.

I believe we should then be far from finding near a fourth part of our Traders single Men *, as is by many with some Probability conjectured; to this Cause I attribute the great Number of Prostitutes of the other Sex, which I believe never can be so effectually remedied, as by making the Marriage State more easy in point of Charge.

And as this will infallibly be effected, by the Means I have pointed out, so it will at the same Time certainly furnish so much more Business of every kind, as considerably to increase the Gains likewise.

Further, when I consider that the Male exceeds the Female Sex about seven in an hundred, by which, if all the Women were in the Marriage State, the fifteenth Man must live single, there being no Female provided for him; and also the natural Modesty of the Female, which being greater, inclines them more strongly to virtuous Love, than the fashionable Bold-ness of the other Sex doth; when I consider these Things, I can find no Cause, to which to impute the 71 great Number of Prostitutes, but || that too many Men avoid the Mariage State, not, as they pretend, for the Sake of being free, and at their Liberty (for in truth they are often wretched Slaves to ill Women and Diseases) but on the Account of the unavoidable

---

* That the single Women are very numerous, will I believe be easily allowed; and then that the Number of single Men are greater is certain, since the Male Sex are considerably more numerous than the Female, as I will presently shew.

and great Charges which attend it, and its being almost impossible to make such Provision for Children, as may put them into as good Circumstances as their Parents began in.

This Motive is indeed so prudent, that I can't help recommending it as the most laudable and praise-worthy Thing in the World, and which I wish both Sexes would always attend to, and be governed by; provided they do at the same time always preserve their Virtue and Innocence unblemished.

The Rules laid down in this Essay are sufficient Direction to the first of these; and for the latter, I must address my self to the fair Sex, and desire them to consider and always remember, that as the great Point of Honour in them is Chastity, so they may see, how wisely Providence hath proportioned the Sexes to maintain it. For as they may assure themselves, the 15th Man through the whole Male Sex, never will, if they can help it, live without a Woman; so the Demand for Women (to speak in the Tradesman's Stile) must necessarily be so great, that they shall not only all have Husbands, if they please, but may refuse too such as they don't so well like, provided they would all be wise and good enough to maintain this their great Point of Honour, Chastity.

And I would hope, it may be a Means to cause some of those, who shall hence be inform || ed, how much 72 more numerous the Male Sex are than the Female, who might otherwise be in any Danger of a dishonourable Surrender, to be more on their Guard, and let no Arts, no Pretences ever prevail, but lawful Marriage, which is, and always will be honourable in all.

And hence we may see, how great an Injury Prostitutes are to Society, since 'tis they only are

the Occasion, that so many Women do and must
live single, and consequently put a great Impediment
on the Increase of the human Race, and cut off a
great deal of Employment from amongst the People,
which depends very much on the Increase of Mankind; and thus they also contribute very much to
make many Women enter on Trades, and work at
Businesses, that should be Employment for Men,
and afford better Wages for the Support of Families,
than any Trades ever will do, where the Women are
considerable Workers at such Trades; and as this
often lays the married Women, whose Business is
to bear Children and guide the House, which is
generally Work enough for them, under a Necessity to work at some Trade or Calling to earn something to help to support their Families, their Husbands Wages being hence insufficient to do it; so
their Children must, and hence often are so neglect-
ed, that many of them are lost, and such of them
as will live almost in spight of such unavoidable
73 Neglects, are commonly Cripples.||

A List of the Males and Females christened in the Bills of Mortality from the Year 1650, to the Year 1689 inclusive, being 40 Years; whence, as it appears the Male Sex exceeds the Female as much as I have asserted; so it is also sufficient to shew there was double the People in the Bills of Mortality at the Year 1689, that there was at the Year 1650; for since the Christenings are more than double, I think it reasonable to conclude the People were doubled, as Dr. Nichols above asserted.

Christened			Christened			Christened		
Anno	Males	Females	Anno	Males	Females	Anno	Males	Females
1650	2890	2722	1666	4678	4319	1682	6909	6744
1	3231	2840	7	5616	5322	3	7577	7158
2	3220	2908	8	6073	5560	4	7575	7127
3	3196	2959	70	6506	5829	5	7484	7246
4	3441	3179	1	6278	5719	6	7575	7119
5	3655	3349	2	6449	6061	7	7737	7214
6	3668	3382	3	6443	6120	8	7487	7101
7	3396	3289	4	6073	5822	9	7604	7167
8	3157	3013	5	6113	5738			
9	3209	2781	6	6058	5717		59948	56876
60	3734	3247	7	6552	5847		99447	93163
1	4748	4107	8	6423	6203		63317	57994
2	5216	4803	9	6568	6033		222712	208033
3	5411	4881	80	6247	6041			208033
4	6041	5681	1	6548	6299			
5	5114	4853		6822	6533			
	63317	57994		99447	93163			

14679 Excess of Males to Females christened in London in 40 Years.

14679) 208033 (14

So that there are about 14 Males to 13 Females, the Excess of Males to Females being about ⅛ Part, which is much about even in an hundred, as I have above asserted; and this Excess is found to be universal, it having been tried in many Cities and Towns all over Europe.

Seventhly, Though what I have been endeavouring to shew through this whole Essay, *viz.* that if the Plenty be made great enough, the Consequence must be both more Employment and Trade too amongst the People; and likewise that the Necessaries of Life, which almost all are ultimately striving for, will be much easier attained, and the People in general thence be in better Circumstances, and a much happier Condition; I say, though these Things suggest themselves with the Clearness and Evidence of first Principles, yet I shall use one Argument more, which will evince, that a vast deal more Business of every Kind, will be the Effect of fully and sufficiently executing this Proposal in all its Parts; and that, from the Consideration of the general Condition and Circumstances of the People, ⅞ of whom, in much better Times of Trade and Business, are, by the Spectator, N° 200, asserted to be without any Property at all in themselves, or the Heads of their Families, and must Work for their daily Bread.

Now ⅞ of so large a Body, as the People of this Kingdom, must needs have a vast Influence on the Trade of it, if we consider them, as being little more than half the Consumers they might and ought to be; which I shall shew, by the following Estimate for a labouring Man and his Family; and though this Estimate is made for a labouring Man's Family in *London*, yet since the Wages of the labouring People in the Country are as much less than Wages in *London*, as the Country People can subsist cheaper, it will still hold that the labouring People 75 in general are but half the Consumers they ought ‖ to be, as the following Estimate will sufficiently prove.

An Estimate of the necessary Charge of a labouring Man and his Family in London, *consisting of a Man and his Wife and four Children, which I take to be a middling Family; however, since they often may have more Children, this must at least be a needful Allowance for a labouring Man and his Family.*

	Daily Expence *per* Head.		Daily Expence of the whole Family.			Weekly Expence of the whole Family.			Yearly Expence of the whole Family.		
	d.	*q.*	*l.*	*s.*	*d.*	*l.*	*s.*	*d.*	*l.*	*s.*	*d.*
Bread for six Persons,		3			4½		2	7½			
Butter,		1			1½			10½			
Cheese,		½			¾			5¼			
Meat,	1				6		3	6			
Small Beer,		2			3		1	9			
Roots, Herbs, Flower, Oatmeal, Salt, Vinegar, Pepper, Mustard, Sugar,		1			1½			10½			
Soap,		½			¾			5¼			
Threads, Needles, Pins, Worsteads, Tapes, &c. for repairing Cloaths, &c.		½			¾			5¼			
Milk one Day with another, for the whole Family,					¾			5¼			
A Candle one Day with another,					¾			5¼			
Coals one Day with another,					2		1	2			
Strong Beer,					1½			10½			
				1	11¾		13	10½			

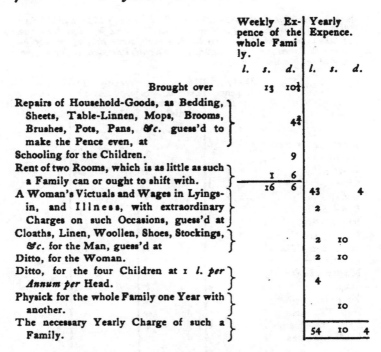

	Weekly Expence of the whole Family.			Yearly Expence.		
	l.	*s.*	*d.*	*l.*	*s.*	*d.*
Brought over		13	10½			
Repairs of Household-Goods, as Bedding, Sheets, Table-Linnen, Mops, Brooms, Brushes, Pots, Pans, &c. guess'd to make the Pence even, at			4¾			
Schooling for the Children.			9			
Rent of two Rooms, which is as little as such a Family can or ought to shift with.		1	6			
		16	6			
A Woman's Victuals and Wages in Lyings-in, and I l l n e s s, with extraordinary Charges on such Occasions, guess'd at				43		4
				2		
Cloaths, Linen, Woollen, Shoes, Stockings, &c. for the Man, guess'd at				2	10	
Ditto, for the Woman.				2	10	
Ditto, for the four Children at 1 *l. per Annum per* Head.				4		
Physick for the whole Family one Year with another.					10	
The necessary Yearly Charge of such a Family.				54	10	4

If any think the Article of Cloaths too much, let them consider to what Purpose the Manufactures are made, if ⅛ of the People can't be allowed to be such inconsiderable Consumers.

And if any think the other Part of the Estimate too large, let them shew how such a Family can with any Decency have their Wants supplied with these Things, cheaper than I have put them.

But if any please to strike any of these Things out of the Estimate, I would advise, that those Things should not be raised in the World at all, since ⅛ of ⁷⁷ Mankind can't be allowed to partake of them. ‖

For high as this Estimate runs, it is not half so much as such a Family will cost in the very next

Station of Life above the labouring Mechanick's Rank, whilst at the same time it's certain, as the Prices of Necessaries now are, the labouring Mechanick can hardly earn enough to purchase half these Things.

For whatever Wages a working Man may sometimes earn, 10 or 12 Shillings *per* Week, when all Deductions are made of lost Time for want of Work and Illness, is the utmost one Man with another can get for himself and Family, which being but 26 or 30 *l. per Annum*, is but about half what is necessary for the Support of such a Family, in the meanest Manner it can be decently done.

This therefore shews the Usefulness and Necessity of making the Plenty so much greater, that every thing may be thereby made much cheaper, that there may be more Work to employ the Poor, and their Wants may be better supplied, which will necessarily make so much more Trade and Business amongst others.

This Estimate also shews, that a Principle I have gone upon, and hitherto taken for granted, is true, in the Nature of the Thing itself, *viz.* that the Wants of Mankind, if fully supplied according to their several Ranks in Life only, are sufficient to give full Employment to all that must get their Living by their Diligence and Labour.

For if ⅓ of the People, were, as they might and ought to be, double the Consumers they are, which, I think, appears by this Estimate; it would rather be a Question, whether Mankind || are able to supply 78 all their Wants, than whether the Wants of Mankind are sufficient to give full Employment to those that want it.

And this is an invincible Argument for a free and unrestrained Trade, since if any Nation makes

Goods for us, we must be making others for them
or some other Nation, and so mutually for each
other, provided our Goods are made cheap enough
to maintain such Commerce.

And if so, what a Number of People will every
Nation thus be able, by means of maritime Commerce, with all its Appendages, to sustain, more
than any such Nation could do, without this Way of
employing and supporting them. For if the People
had not this Way to employ them, they must fall
into Agriculture for Employment; in which Case,
the same Number of People would require a vastly
greater Extent of Territory to support them, than
in the former Case; and their Affluence * would in
general be vastly less likewise; besides, that such a
Nation would not be near so formidable; the Reasons
of which I shall endeavour to shew.

If any certain Quantity of Land well cultivated
and improved will produce Corn and Cattle, and
all other Necessaries for the Use of Man, when only
⅓ of the People, suppose, are immediately employ'd
this Way, whilst the other ⅔ are employed in mari-
79 time Affairs, and Affairs thereunto re ‖ lating, and
otherVocations; if the People can be so subsisted, as
they undoubtedly are, at the same Time that their
maritime Commerce is not only so useful, to employ
so very great a Part of them, as subsist in any Relation to it, but brings them Gold and Silver, who
have no other Way to procure any amongst them,
which Gold and Silver, by being made the Medium
of all Transactions, circulates swiftly through every

---

* To convince us of this, we need only compare the Magnificence and
Splendour of a City or Town, whose maritime Trade is considerable, with
the Rusticity and Meanness of the Country People; for let them set up
Coaches, and build fine Seats, as many Merchants and Tradesmen in
such Towns are continually doing, and then I'll acknowledge that Affluence and Power are so immediately connected with the Plow, that no Nation need concern themselves at all about maritime Commerce.

Hand, in suitable Proportion to the Business each
Particular transacts, leaving also amongst many of
them a Surplus, greater than what their particular
Occasions require, which constitutes the Wealth of
such Particulars, and which, when many of the People
are thus enriched, constitutes what is called national
Affluence; I say, a Nation doth thus become properly
affluent, and that includes Strength and Power.

All Interruptions therefore of this Commerce,
whilst it continues gainful (*i. e.* increases the Nation's Cash) will no doubt be allowed to lessen
this Affluence, Strength and Power. Therefore when
any Branch of Commerce lessens the Cash of a
Nation, I expect it will be thought fit by high Duties
or Prohibitions to restrain or suppress it; but this
I shall take the Liberty to deny, because it will hence
become fit for other Nations to lay such Restraints
or Prohibitions, as never to let us have a gainful
Trade, if they can help it, it being just so far a losing Trade to them as it's gainful to us; and as maritime Commerce must be, and certainly now is, very
much lessened by these mutual Restraints, so many
People must have lost their Employment in every
such Nation, and where they will find || Employment, 80
but in Tillage and Cultivation of Land, I can't imagine; wherefore, if they must employ such, or an
equal Number of others this Way, which indeed the
rising Generation will best and most naturally supply
for that Purpose, as they can't be employed on the
Land before cultivated, so it's certain they must have
so much larger Territory to support the same Number of People, whereby, as their domestick Trade
will languish as their maritime Trade decreases,
because domestick Trade doth very much depend
on maritime Trade, so their maritime Force will
decrease together with them; for the Truth of which,

6

I appeal to Experience and Fact, whether every Nation be not more or less formidable, as their maritime Commerce is more extensive or less considerable; whence it's plain, Affluence and Strength are so connected with the maritime Trade of a Nation, that they must increase or diminish together.

But if every Nation, instead of such Restraints, would make their Produce, &c. cheap enough, which they can always do, and that to the real Advantage of every Part of the Community, their good and cheap Goods would force themselves by these Qualities (which are inseparably connected) on some other Nations at least, and, I think, on them too who endeavour to restrain them, and thus extend as well as preserve their maritime Commerce, and with it their Affluence and Prowess.

And this might perhaps demonstrate to others the Folly of restraining Trade in any Degree whatsoever, and be a Means to point the Way to make 81 their People happy in Trade without ‖ such Restraints, or ever going to War with each other about it; for War, I am sure, is always in its Consequences, as destructive of Trade as it is of the Peace and Happiness of Mankind.

But the above Estimate shews, that if the Produce of the Earth were doubled, it would certainly be consumed, since the Wages of the labouring People, who are the Bulk of Mankind *, are not sufficient to purchase above half the Necessaries such a Family doth require. If it be said, every one hath not so large a Family; I answer, that many have larger; and as it is reasonably expected, every Man should provide for his own Family, how large soever it may be; it hence becomes fit, that every Man should be

---

* The labouring People being so great a Part of the whole as ⅞, for Argument Sake, I take them here for the whole.

capable to earn, at least, as much as will provide for such a middling Family, as the Estimate is made for.

But I must observe, that the Produce of the Earth could not be doubled, unless the Quantity of Land in Use were also doubled; for the Land in Use doth certainly, generally, produce as much as it can well be made to bear; therefore it follows, there must be twice as much Land to bear twice the present Quantity of Produce, which the Estimate shews would be consumed, without altering the several Ranks and Stations of Man in any Respect, but that of being comfortably supported in the several Ranks and Stations of Life. .

But to double the Produce, there must be double the Number of People employed in Cul || tivation 82 of Land. Now, I think it self-evident, that Trade, Manufactures, &c. could not possibly spare half such a Number of People out of them, without making Trade, Manufactures, &c. much too profitable, and encouraging, to suffer half so many People to employ themselves any other Way. For as it is the Demand, which governs and fixes the Price of every thing, if so many People were to be taken out of Trade, Manufactures, &c. as half the Quantity of Land,.we have now in Use, would require to cultivate and improve it, and go through all the Parts of Business arising thereby, the Manufacturers, Traders, &c. would undoubtedly be able to exact almost what Price they pleased for their Work and Business. Upon the whole then, we may see, that all the Produce of the Earth and Manufactures would be wanted and used, if Things were to be put on so happy a Foot, as I am pointing out; and that the Wants of Mankind are full as great, as both their Abilities, and the Earth too, are.capable of supplying; whence it follows, that any Want of Employment or Trade amongst the People, is solely owing to this, that we have not Land enough in Use to employ and support them.

Again, I would observe, that if the present Quantity of Produce were to be augmented only one Fourth at most (and perhaps People enough might be spared out of Trade, Manufactures, &c. to do this) it would certainly fall the Price of the Produce half.

For since Farms must, in this Case, be one Fourth 83 more numerous than they are, the Rents || of Lands would thereby necessarily be considerably lowered; and if the Produce of the Earth would, in this Case, be augmented to so great a Degree, as a fourth Part also, as I suppose it certainly would; these Things taken together, I think, could not fail to lower the Price of the Produce half, and then Labour would of Necessity be lowered also, because the working People would be under no less Necessity than they are now, to work as cheap as they possibly can.

For if, as it hath been shewn, the Produce can't be doubled, to enable the working People to be double the Consumers they now are, as the Estimate shews they certainly would, if they could get it, and that without bringing them at all out of the Rank and Condition of working People: Nay, if the Produce can't be increased half, nor perhaps hardly one Fourth neither, would not absolute Necessity oblige the working People to work as cheap as they possible can, that they may be able to supply their Wants as far as they can, which yet, it appears by the Estimate, must be considerably abridged, notwithstanding the Plenty, which a fourth Part more Land than we now have in Use would produce; and notwithstanding too, that there would, in this Case, be so much more Employment for the working People, as would fill up the whole Time they have to labour in: So true is the Proverb, and so true 'twill always be, That nothing is cheap, but poor Folks Labour.

But this Estimate shews, how much the Necessaries of Life ought to be lowered in Price, in order to reduce the Wages of the labouring ||People, so as to 84 make much more Employment for them, and at the same time increase the Consumption of every thing to such a Degree, that there may be a great deal more Business amongst the trading Part of the People.

The labouring People, I am sure, and do insist on it, notwithstanding my Estimate, can make about 16 Shillings *per* Week support such a Family, as the Estimate is made for, though I know not, nor desire to know, how to make an Estimate thereof; and I have heard them that have such Families, declare they should think themselves happy, if they could get so much one Week with another; wherefore it appears to me, that in order to reduce Labour, the Necessaries of Life should be lowered about half, that 8 Shillings might purchase as much as 16 will now do; and then Labour might be lowered at least one Fourth, and the labouring People be enabled, notwithstanding, to purchase near half as many more Necessaries as their present Wages of 10 or 12 Shillings *per* Week will do, at the Rates these Things now go; and, I think, any one who considers the Pittances allowed in the Estimate, must think it fit, that the labouring People, if they will be industrious, should notwithstanding any manner of Pretences or Suggestions to the contrary, have it in their Power to obtain half as many more Necessaries for their Support and Comfort, as their present

Wages will now purchase, and then there would be almost half as much more Trade and Business amongst the People in general, as there now is, or
85 can be till this be done; || besides all other mighty Advantages, inseparably connected with it; of which, the Removal of many of those Temptations, which contribute to the Destruction of the Poor, and which would, in this Case, in a great Measure be certainly removed, is no small one.

For I take the great Number of Brandy-shops and Ale-houses, which have multiplied so mightily of late Years, to be one of the greatest Snares and Temptations that could be laid in the Way of the labouring People, and which introduces most of the Calamities and Vices they fall into; these which are so great a Snare to the poorer Sort, as Taverns also are to many in better Stations, would, I think, soon be very much reduced in their Numbers (though I suppose we shall always have enough of them) if so much new Employment were produced for the People in general, as would arise by the Execution of this Proposal.   7

For since it hath been shewn, that the full Execution of this Proposal will create as much Employment and Trade as the People can possibly perform, I think the trading People would soon find more honourable, if not more profitable Ways to subsist, than by enticing and encouraging the working People to spend the Money they know should be saved for and laid out on their Families; and instead of suffering them to disorder themselves, and waste that Time, which should be employed to gain a Support for their Families, or if they have none, to provide against the Infirmities of Age, and other
86 Accidents of Life, or for near and helpless Relati- || ons, they would even turn such disorderly People

out of their Houses, or at least not sell them Liquors so vastly injurious to them, and all the Relations they stand in to others. For there are Instances of Brandy-Shops and Publick-houses, who having pretty good Trades will not suffer such Excesses in their Houses, notwithstanding the many Examples, and State of Trade in general are bad enough to justify any Means of attaining a Livelihood, not absolutely unlawful. But there is a Necessity to lower the Necessaries of Life to about half the present Price, if we would reduce Labour only one fourth Part lower than it now goes; for as it is the Demand alone, which gives the Value, and fixes the Price to every thing, any slender Attempts to employ the Poor, and make more Business this Way arise to others, would by encreasing the Demand for Labour, &c. rather tend to raise the Wages of the labouring People, and augment the Profits of the trading Part, than to lower either of them; for I believe the trading People in general (and their numerous Complaints to the Parliament, shew as much, as well as an Estimate I have subjoined) stand in need of larger Profits, as the first Estimate also shews the labouring People do of larger Supplies, than their present Wages will now procure them.

But perhaps it may be asked, How Labour can be reduced the Way I propose, since the Demand for it (which always advances the Price of every thing) will be greater: To which I answer, that it is the present Rates of Labour only that ‖ will be re-87 duced my Way, but its Value, according to the above Maxim will be greater, when the Necessaries of Life are rendered so much cheaper, that a fourth Part less Wages will purchase near half as many more Necessaries as the present Rates of Labour will do; and as this is all the Reduction of Labour I am aiming at, or which in the Nature of the Thing is possible, so, that I may be clearly understood, let it be supposed, that such a labouring Man's Family can be decently maintained (as it most certainly may) with about 16 Shillings *per* Week, and that the Necessaries of Life were lowered to half their present Price; as 8 Shillings would then purchase as much as 16 will now do, which is at least a third more than their present Wages of 10 or 12 Shillings will now purchase; so Labour would then really be about ⅓ Part more valuable than it is now, though its Rate at the same time be lowered about ⅓ Part also.

But if we would really effect this, we must undoubtedly, as fast as possible, improve such large Tracts of waste Land, as will employ all the Hands, Trade, and Manufactures will possibly suffer to be employed this Way; for a Nation is a great Body of People, and if we would do Things they may all feel the good Effects of, we must do great Things indeed; and a very great Thing it will be to reduce the Price of Necessaries half, which, I think, I have shewn to be absolutely needful to reduce the present Rates of Labour, and at the same time supply the labouring People with the Things needful to that Station of Life, and thereby make so much more Business 88 amongst others, without ‖ which, Trade in general cannot flourish, because all Trade depends solely on the Consumption; and yet, I think it appears, by what I have said, that Trade will flourish, before the Poor will find in their Power to attain the Supplies I wish them, since the Labour of the Poor is the Wealth of the Rich; and if it was unreasonable to muzzle the Ox that trod out the Corn, what Name shall I give the Measures that render it so difficult for the Bulk of Mankind, to answer the great End of Life, that of raising Families to stand in their

Room when they are removed, as all soon must be
to give Place to succeeding Generations?

But there is another Thing, which would mightily
contribute to the Reduction of Labour, which is, the
bringing Fish out of the Sea at such cheap Rates,
as that the Poor might be induced, by its being
cheaper than Meat, to make it a good Part of their
common Food; and as we are inviron'd by the Sea,
which will furnish never the less, how much soever
we fetch thence; beside, that this Food requires no
Land, except to grow the Timber, &c. to build the
Vessels with; and this Food is no sooner caught,
but it is fit for Use, and therefore requires neither
the Time nor Labour, that all other Food Mankind
use requires, to raise, and fit it for Use; I say, since
we are inviron'd with the Sea, we might certainly
bring Fish so cheap to a Multitude of inland Places,
if the Charge of catching them, and Carriage could
be very much lessened, as would make it a much
larger Part of the Food of the common People
than it is. || 89

But though this will, in the first Place, somewhat
depend on the Reduction of Labour, yet I apprehend it to depend as much at least on making
Timber so plentiful, that, if possible, the Charge of
the Vessels they fish with, may be lessened about
half in building, and fitting them to Sea; for the
greatest Part of the Price of Fish, is constituted of
the Charge of building and maintaining the fishing
Vessels and Tackle, together with the Interest of
the Sums such Vessels, &c. cost, which are employed
in the Fishery. Wherefore could these Charges be
considerably lessened, which a great Plenty of
Timber, &c. with somewhat cheaper Rate of Labour
would certainly effect, we might make Sea Fish so
much cheaper Food than Meat, as would contribute

very much to lowering the Price of Provisions in general, and might hereby support a much greater Number of People on less Land than we can otherwise do; and it's certain the *Dutch*, who have about two Millions and an half of People, upon about a Million of Acres of Land, do by this Means, besides others, very much contribute to the supporting such a vastly greater Number of People in respect of their small Territory, than we, who have but about eight Millions of People, and hardly less than twenty Millions of Acres now in Use to support them*; besides, that such an Encouragement‖ to our Fishery would be a most useful Nursery for able Seamen, and a Benefit in respect of our Exportation of Fish, greater than I shall attempt to represent.

But this Estimate further shews, that the fit Rule to judge and determine when the Necessaries of Life should be denominated cheap or dear, is solely that of the general Earnings or Wages of the labouring People, which undoubtedly ought to be such as will procure so many of those Things as are needful to support such Families, as is the Lot of

---

* *Benjamin Motte's* Philosophical Transactions abridged,[11] Part 4. Page 24. demonstrate *England* or *South Britain* to contain 72,000 square Miles, or 46,800,000 Acres; he also says, the Province of *Holland* is computed to contain about a Million of Acres, which is said to contain 2,400,000 Souls, so that *England*, to be proportionably populous, must have 110 Millions of People; but he says, to allow Room enough for Persons of all Degrees under our *British* Monarchy, if *England* were half as populous as *Holland*, with only 55 Millions of People, it were a good Proportion, and would be near five times our present Number; so that according to him, we must have about eleven Millions of People in *England*.

He further says, that to people *England* with this Number, *viz.* 55 Millions, there are sundry Ways very practicably, by which he hath computed, the present Number may be doubled in 24 or 25 Years, and probably quadrupled in about 36 Years; but I think *England* is not capable to sustain double its present Number of Inhabitants, because it is undoubtedly at present above half cultivated and improved, yet I think I have made it evident, we have not near Land enough in Use to support its present Inhabitants.

Dr. *John Lawrence* in his new System of Agriculture, Page 45, says, 'tis believed that almost one half Part of the Kingdom is Commons.

many of the labouring People to have. From hence
therefore we may also see, when Money is, or is not
sufficiently plentiful amongst the People in general,
or which is equivalent thereto, when there is, or is
not Land enough in Use to support them, for hence
only can these Things be brought and kept near together, as is absolutely needful to put the Affairs of
the World, and Condition of Mankind in the best
and happiest Situation they can possibly be in.

For whilst a Mechanick, or labouring Man can't
possibly earn so much, as will provide de ‖ cently for 91
a middling Family, suitably to that low Rank of
Life; it's plain, Money, which is the sole Medium of
procuring any Thing, is so much too scarce amongst
⅞ of the People at least; or which, as I said, is the
same Thing in Effect, that there is not Land enough
in Use to support them, and consequently, there is
in this Case, so much less Business and Employment amongst the People in general, than there
ought to be; whence the Distress of great Numbers
is unavoidable: And Gentlemen should consider, if
⅞ of the People must labour under the Penury this
Estimate holds forth to them, what a Probability
here is, that many of their own Offspring, in a Generation or two, if not much sooner, will find themselves in no better Circumstances.

And hence I can't help reflecting how good human
Nature is, that can support under the Hardships,
we, by the Estimate, see the Bulk of Mankind lies
under; which Hardships, I think, I have now sufficiently shewn, cannot be any Way justly attributed
to the all-wise and infinitely gracious Creator, but
solely to those, who for want of thus looking thro'
the Nature of Things, and from a mistaken Judgment, that the more Money they receive for their
Estates, the richer they are (the contrary of which

I have proved) do prevent the People from thus continually proceeding in the Business of Cultivation and Tillage, whence alone every thing they have is derived, and whence only whatsoever they want can be supplied, and whence all the Employment and Trade of the World do proceed; and to which End 92 it was, that Man was sent || into the World, as I shall further confirm, by the Authority of the Holy Scriptures, *Gen.* iii. 23. *Therefore the Lord God sent him forth to till the Ground whence he was taken.*

But I shall proceed to shew from Fact, that it is the Interest of the landed Gentlemen to cause so much more Land to be added and improved, as will effect the Things I am aiming at, by comparing the present Rents of Lands, and Prices of Necessaries, with the Rents of Lands, and Prices of Necessaries some Centuries ago.

Now though the Rents of Lands are very different, according as the Soil or Situation is better or worse *, yet it's certain the present Rents of Lands in general are hardly four times as much as they were about four Centuries ago; but the Prices of Necessaries differ vastly: For the Price of the fat Ox, which was a Noble, is now about 10 or 12 Pounds; the fat Sheep, which was 6 Pence, is now about 16 Shillings; the fat Goose, which was 2 Pence, is now about 3 Shillings; the fat Pig, which was 1 Penny, is now about 4 Shillings; the Price of 6 Pidgeons, which was 1 Penny, is now about 1 Shilling and 6 Pence; and Wheat, which was 2 Shillings *per* Quarter, is now about 24 or 26

---

* If we take the Rents of good Lands in *England*, at a Medium, to be about 10 Shillings *per* Acre, and the Rents of bad Lands, at a Medium, to be about two Shillings and Sixpence *per* Acre, and that their Quantities are near equal, then the Rents of Lands will be about 6 Shillings *per* Acre now at a Medium; and as far as I can learn 6 or 7 Shillings *per* Acre at Medium, is as much as the Lands of *England* are now worth; and I believe I may be bold to say, the Lands of *England*, at a Medium, have not let for less than one Shilling and Six-pence *per* Acre for four hundred Years backwards.

Shillings *per* Quarter; and all other Things differ in such Proportion. Whence it appears, these || Things 93 are now higher in Price then they were then, from about 20 to 30 Times and upwards, except Wheat, which I suppose *Eras. Phillips*, Esq; in his State of the Nation, *&c.* Page 52. accounts for, where he says, It's observable, Corn hath not risen in proportion to other Commodities, because by a new-fashioned Industry the same Quantity of Ground is more productive than it was. Therefore it's plain in fact that Gentlemen are vast Losers by this Advance of their Rents, since they, in common with all other Consumers, now pay on the Par above 20 times as much for every thing as was paid for the same Things about four Centuries ago, whilst their Rents are not above four times as much as they were then; therefore it must be mightily for the Interest of the landed Gentlemen, to cause Land enough to be added and improved, to put Trade into a flourishing State, since it must be equally certain, that every thing will fall in as much greater Proportion than the Rents will fall, as it's certainly Fact, every thing is risen in so much greater Proportion than the Rents have been raised.

But I can't pass over this Fact without remarking, that it must be beneficial to Trade, that our Princes, Nobility, and Gentry, should wear the richest Gold and Silver Cloathing, and use such Utensils, and adorn their Palaces and Houses with these shining Metals, as much as the Revenues of the Crown, or Income of the Estates of the Nobility and Gentry will admit; only with this Difference, that crowned Heads may lay out this Way, whatever the Extent of their Revenues will allow; but the Nobility and || 94 Gentry must act in this, with such Regard to their Families, that they may all be properly provided for, whilst the Heir only should fill up such splendid Appearances.

The Reason of which is this, that it appears plainly from this Discourse, that as the Gold and Silver (*i. e.* Money) increases in greater Proportion than the People increase, so will the Prices of every thing advance, and that in much greater Proportion than the Rents will or can rise; wherefore it can't but be beneficial even for Trade, that as much of these Metals be used in Splendor, as is consistent with the abovementioned Circumstances; because by thus keeping so much of those Metals out of Trade, the more just Distinction will it keep up amongst the several Ranks and Stations of Men *, whilst at the same time it will give so much greater Employment, and that in the most nice and curious Arts, to Mechanicks, *&c.* and prevent our Markets from rising so high, as to hinder the Exportation of our Commodities, or give too great Encouragement to the Importation of foreign Goods.

I am induced to make this Remark, from the Practice of the *East-Indians*, who, as I have often heard, carry this Matter so far, as to bury the Money 95 they get by Trade; as *E. Phillips*, || Esq; Page 7. also says, that they have since the Year 1602, buried above 150 Millions of Silver, which hath been brought 96 into *Europe*†. ||

---

* Money is the Tradesman's working Tools, without which he can't proceed in Trade at all; therefore, since the Increase of Money amongst the People will increase the Price of Things in greater Proportion than the Rents can be raised, the more Money circulates in Trade, the more must the Traders have in their Hands to carry it on; and this will necessarily raise Tradesmen so much nearer the Rank of Gentry, as the Quantity of Cash they circulate is greater in Proportion to the Rents, than it would be if the Prices of Things were kept lower, the Way above suggested.

† I would by no means have us follow their Example of burying our Money, any further, than that every Man should be his own Banker, that is, I would have no publick Banking any ways encouraged; nor any Companies ever incorporated; because, besides many Evils that necessarily adhere

'Tis by this Practice they keep all their Goods and Manufactures at such low Rates, that all *Europe* thinks it not only worth while to trade with them, but to carry prodigious Quantities of Silver* to

to all trading Corporations, their Stock and Bonds have the same Effects as Banking, *viz.* operating two Ways at the same time, in their Trade, and in our Markets; so that any thing can always be bought with them, just as if such Paper were Gold and Silver; I say, I would therefore have none of these Things encouraged; and then if Property were but sufficiently diffused amongst the People in general, we might sleep very safe with large Sums under slender Fastenings; for it is Necessity which makes Thieves.

Now if every Man were his own Banker, and Trade put on so good a Foot, as to diffuse Property so effectually, that every industrious and prudent Tradesman, though his Circumstances were not great, might get Money, there would soon be Millions locked up in the Hands of the People of this Kingdom; and as this is the fit and natural Way of burying Money, so this would reduce the Price of our Goods below the Rates, which the Cash, if it were all afloat, would support them at; and which now by Banking and other artificial Moneys, *i. e.* Paper Effects having the Operation of Money, are certainly, vastly above the Rates which the real Specie itself, which we have now amongst us, would support them at.

But perhaps the Merchants may object, they can't do so much Business without more Hands, if there were no Banking at all; to which I answer, that such as have so much Business as to require a Hand the more on that Account, must employ one; yet I will mention a Practice in *Holland* well known to many of our Merchants. The Merchants in *Holland*, frequently make large Payments in a coarse, and therefore a bulky Sort of Specie, called Ses d'Halve, which they deliver each other in Bags unopened, containing 375 Guldens, and numbered, or ticketed without Side so many, and also weighing so much, which they may tell over at home if they please, and if any thing is found short, the Merchant that paid it, on telling him how much it fell short, immediately, without any Questions, makes it good; and if there be an Overplus, they always reckon themselves obliged to carry that Overplus to the Owner. This honourable Way of dealing in the valuable Article of Money, may possibly seem strange to us, who are not used to it; but I believe if we had no Banking, and our Specie were as coarse and bulky as theirs, the Merchants would soon find it convenient to introduce this Practice amongst them, and no doubt would discharge it as honourably; and then large Payments might be made almost as quick as Draughts on the Bankers with the Entries they occasion, and the necessary Settlements with the Bankers about them afterwards; besides, that the vast Damage arising by Failure of Bankers, would this Way be intirely prevented.

* The *Indians* are so politick, as to take only or chiefly Silver, because it's next to impossible it should ever be so plentiful, as to reduce its Value in respect of Gold, which to be sure they know too to be continually growing so plentiful in *Europe*, as to lower its Value in respect of Silver; besides Silver being of so much less Value than Gold can't be much diminished but it will be obvious; nor is there near the Temptation to counterfeit it.

What is it therefore, which infatuates us and other Nations to such a Degree, as to carry the *Indians* almost all our Silver? The Author of the

purchase their Commodities, whilst our Goods cannot possibly find much Vend with them, being so much dearer than theirs, as we see the great Circulation of Gold amongst us, makes our Goods in respect of the Prices of theirs, who this Way prevent the Money they gain by Trade from raising the Prices of their Commodities.

Thus will they not only always preserve the Balance of Trade in their Favour, but make many other Nations carry their Money to them; besides what Use they may make of such immense Wealth, if any Exigence or Design should oblige them to use it; which Wealth is as many times more power-97 ful to them than it ‖ would be to us, as the Wages of their labouring People are lower than ours.

But an Objection arises here, which though it allows, that if all the Things our Gentry consume and use were our own natural Produce, they would, as I have proved, be the richer for executing this Proposal; yet since they consume so many foreign Goods, as perhaps constitute half their Expence, *viz.* Teas, Sugars, Fruits, Linens, Cambrick, Laces, Wines, *&c.* the Prices of which depend so much on what they cost at the Places they are brought from, that they can receive but little Alteration by the Execution of this Proposal; the Gentry therefore will not be the richer for such a Reduction of Labour, and Prices of our natural Produce, as would hereby be effected.

To which I answer, That all Nations have some Commodities peculiar to them, which therefore are

Plan of the *English* Commerce, 2d Edition printed 1730,[12] will answer this Question for me; for Page 65, he says, *China* and *India*, and other Eastern Countries have the most extended Manufactures, and the greatest Variety of them in the World; and their Manufactures push themselves on the World by the meer Stress of their Cheapness, which causes their Consumption; and Page 66, he says, the Wages of their labouring People do not exceed two Pence Sterling *per* Day.

undoubtedly designed to be the Foundation of
Commerce between the several Nations, and pro-
duce a great deal of Employment by maritime
Affairs, &c. for Mankind, which probably, without
such Peculiarities, could not be; and in this Respect,
I suppose we are distinguished, as well as other
Nations; and I have before taken Notice, that if one
Nation be by Nature more distinguished in this
Respect than another, as they will by that Means
gain more Money than such other Nations, so the
Prices of all their Commodities and Labour will be
higher in such Proportion, as my fourth Maxim
demonstrates; and consequently, they will not be a
Jot the richer or more powerful for having more
Money than their Neighbours. || 98

But if we import any kind of Goods cheaper than
we can now raise them, which otherwise might as
well be raised at home; in this Case, undoubtedly,
'tis indispensably necessary for us to practise the
Method I prescribe, which is the only one, by which
we ever can be enabled to raise all such Commodities at home, and thereby furnish so many new
Branches of Employment and Trade for our own
People, and remove the Inconvenience of receiving
any Goods from abroad, which we can any ways
raise on as good Terms our selves; and as this should
be done to prevent every Nation from finding their
Account with us, by any such Commodities whatsoever, so this would more effectually shut out all such
foreign Goods than any Law can do.

And as this is all the Prohibition and Restraint,
whereby any foreign Trade should be obstructed,
so if this Method be continually observed and practised, as it most certainly ought, our Gentry would
find themselves the richer, notwithstanding their
Consumption of such other foreign Goods, as being

7

the Peculiarities of other Nations, we may be obliged
to import. For if, when we have increased our Produce to so great a Degree, as to reduce the Rates
of Labour considerably too, and have thereby enabled ourselves to raise many Kinds of Goods, which
we now import, cheaper than we now import them,
which is the necessary Consequence of executing
this Proposal; I say, when we have thus raised all
we can at home, and thereby put our Trade into a
flourishing State, the Goods we import after this is
99 done, being cheaper ‖ than we can raise such Goods
ourselves, which they must be, or we shall not import them; I say, it's plain the Consumption of any
such Goods cannot occasion so great an Expence,
as they would if we could shut them out, by an Act
of Parliament, to raise them ourselves. If therefore
it would be true, as the Objection allows, that the
Gentry would be the richer for executing this Proposal, if all the Goods they consume and use were
the natural Produce of our own Country, they must
be so, notwithstanding their Consumption of any
Quantity of foreign Goods, which we can import and
sell at cheaper Rates than we can possibly raise
them ourselves; for none but such cheaper foreign
Goods, can ever find a Vend in any Nation, except
they be the Peculiarities of other foreign Nations;
to which I have given a full Answer above.

From hence therefore it must appear, that it is
impossible any body should be the poorer, for using
any foreign Goods at cheaper Rates than we can
raise them ourselves, after we have done all we
possibly can to raise such Goods as cheap as we
import them, and find we cannot do it; nay this very
Circumstance makes all such Goods come under the
Character of the Peculiarities of those Countries,
which are able to raise any such Goods cheaper than
we can do; for they will necessarily operate as such.

8*thly*, The full and sufficient Execution of this
Proposal, is the only Means by which Property can
be reasonably and sufficiently diffused amongst all
Ranks of People. For whilst the working People
have not sufficient and full Em || ployment *, their 100
Labour, like all other Things, whose Quantity is
greater than the Demand for them, must be disposed
of below its true and just Value; which I have shewn
is, or ought to be, as near as possible, so much as
will produce a comfortable Subsistence for a Family,
suitable to that Rank of Life: Now so long as these
in general work so considerably below this Point,
that their Wages are generally insufficient to support
such a Family, as the Estimate supposes them to
have, Property is evidently not so much diffused, as
in the Nature and Reason of Things it ought to be;
which will necessarily be attended with many Kinds
of Evils, in Proportion to the Degree, which the
working Peoples Wages fall short of the Point
abovementioned: For hence the Wealthy having
the working Peoples Labour and Skill so much too
cheap, do not only engross that Property, in which
the labouring People have a just and natural Right,
so far as their Wages fall short of the End aforesaid,
but they hereby accumulate a great deal of Wealth,
in which the middling People have a reasonable and
natural Property; and many of them who understand
Trade, are enabled by the Force of such unequal
Wealth, to trade on Terms too low to admit many
of the middling People to get a Livelihood, suitable

* If there were full Employment for the working People, their Wages
would as certainly rise to the just Value of Labour, as we know every thing
else doth, for which the Demand is equal to the Quantity; and therefore
I deny that there is Work enough to employ the People, or that Property
is reasonably or sufficiently diffused, till Necessaries are rendered so plentiful, and thereby so cheap, that the Wages of the labouring Man will purchase as many of them as the decent and comfortable Support of a middling
Family requires in that Station of Life.

101 to their Rank and || Station: For instance, suppose a Man in Trade worth 10000 *l.* and the Reduction of Interest hath actually brought too many such into several Retail Trades; I say, suppose such a one, in order to turn his Stock once in the Year, will vend his Goods at 10 *per Cent.* profit, this will produce 1000 *l. per Annum*; now let another in the same Way of Trade worth 1000 *l.* sell at the same Rate (as he must, or have very little Business) and let him be supposed (because a less Stock may commonly be oftener return'd than a greater) to turn his Stock twice a Year; which, since giving Credit is become so general, is as often as such a Stock in Retail Trade can generally be returned; this though it produces 20 *l. per Cent.* on this Capital, or 200 *l. per Annum*, shall hereafter be shewn to be very insufficient to bear all Charges of Trade, and support a middling Family, so as it is undoubtedly reasonable such a Family should live, for whose Support 1000 *l.* of their own Money is employed in Trade: Whilst the other making 10 *per Cent.* on his large Capital, may still more and more encrease it, at the same time that he is bringing on the Ruin of many that have but middling Capitals. Hence therefore it must appear, that not only the labouring Mechanicks, but many of the middling People must with them be dispossessed of that Property, which their Rank in Life, and the Good of the Community, naturally intitle them too, for that Community will always be most powerful, and most happy, that abounds most with middling People; and as there is no Means, by which Property can be diffused amongst the People 102 in || general, except that I am pointing out, so I think it self-evident, that this Means cannot fail of diffusing Property, amongst all Ranks of People, to such a Degree, as that all, that will be industrious,

and careful, may be comfortably supported according to the several Ranks and Stations, in which Providence may think fit to cast them; and whenever Property is thus diffused, it is not only sufficiently diffused, but involves all the Happiness the Nature of Things is capable of producing to Mankind; so that whatever Difference there shall then be in the Circumstances, Conditions, and Ranks of Men, they will only be such as the Author of Nature designed, and such as are inseparably connected with civil Government, in which there must necessarily be high and low, as long as Government subsists.

9thly, The full and sufficient Execution of this Proposal, is the only natural or possible Means, by which Luxury, so far as it is injurious to Society, can be removed.

I don't call that State, Equipage, or Way of Living, which is suitable to the Rank or Condition of a Man, Luxury hurtful to Society, how pompous soever, if it be contained within the Limits of his Estate, to such a Degree, as will admit of his making such Provision for his Family, as his Rank and Dignity requires; for I think such State and Way of Living necessary and useful to Society, whilst it's confined within the Bounds aforesaid.

Therefore as that Man only can be called luxurious, in a Sense hurtful to Society, who exceeds these Bounds; so a Nation only can be || said to be luxurious, when the People too generally exceed in this Respect. That this may possibly be the Case of a Nation, I shall take for granted, and admit, that one must be reduced to Distress, as sure as the other.

Now the Cause of such general or national Luxury, is solely owing to too great an Inequality of Property, by which too many are enabled to live excessively splendid, whilst the rest, having much less than they want, are too much depress'd and sunk; so that whilst one Side are almost adored for their Wealth, the other are almost abhorred for their Poverty; and as this makes the Gap much too wide between these Extreams, it can't be expected, but that the adored Part of Mankind will necessarily be imitated, beyond proper Limits, by most of those between these Extreams; and this compleats the Notion of Luxury hurtful to Society.

But were Property to be so diffused, as I have shewn it may and ought, the Labour, &c. of the People would not come on Terms so unreasonably low, as to support such Excess on the one Hand, or to depress and sink the rest too much on the other: Nay, diffusing Property as aforesaid, will not only remove Luxury so far as it is hurtful to Society, but will in general extinguish all Kinds of Vice together with it. For this too great Inequality of Property, I have now represented, is the sole Source, whence they all spring; and *Solomon*, the wisest of Men, hath determined this of the Poor, who are the Bulk of Mankind, when he says, as in the Motto I have chosen to this Essay; *The Destruction of the* 104 *Poor is their Poverty*. But sure, Destruction || was never justly attributed to any other Cause than Vice; wherefore Poverty and Vice must according to *Solomon* be necessarily connected; and, I think, Excess of Affluence must be so too, since it is but changing *Solomon*'s Determination to the other Extream.

But that I may fully prove, that the Execution of this Proposal will certainly remove Luxury, so far as it's hurtful to Society, which is all the Concern we need in the present Case have about it; I assert, that a middling Family in *London*, will in a very

moderate Way of Living, in the middling Station of
Life, require about 400 *l. per Annum* to maintain
and make Provision for them, as by a subsequent
Estimate shall be made appear: Now this Sum is
undoubtedly as much more than the People in the
middling Rank of Life can generally get, as the
Wages of the labouring People are less than the
Estimate for such a Family shews to be needful;
therefore I insist, as I have before shewn, that if the
Produce of the Ground were augmented about half,
the Wants of the People are great enough to consume it all, and that without living in the least luxu-   ᵗ˒
riously; since by both Estimates it appears, only
necessary Things are allowed for the two Stations
of Life, in which almost all Mankind are included.
For the Number of those above the lower and middling Stations, are undoubtedly few in Comparison
to the Numbers, which must be included within the
Bounds of these Estimates: If therefore the Produce
of the Earth would be wanted and consumed, though
it were augmented to so great a Degree as half;
and if, as I have before shewn, || it is perhaps not ₁₀₅
possible to increase it so much; and if, however,
what we can do to augment it makes Plenty, and
the Nature of Plenty be such as necessarily to bring
those Things into the Power of the middling and
lower People, who are those only that stand in need
of them; if these Things are so, how is it possible
there should be any general or national Luxury   ᴵᵛ
amongst the People, since we can't make the Earth
produce so much as will support or cause it? Nay,   ᴵᵛ
since the Method of increasing the Produce, naturally and necessarily diffuses the Increase amongst
the lower and middling People who alone want it;
it must be plain, that this must remove Luxury, so
far as it's hurtful to Society; and also, that Luxury

is founded in too great an Inequality of Property, as I have asserted: And hence also it must appear, that Luxury is not the Cause but the Effect of a Decay of Trade, since a Decay of Trade is nothing else but the Bulk of the Peoples wanting many Things, which they ought to have, and which, for want of sufficient Employment and Business, it is out of their Power to procure.

10*thly*, The full and sufficient Execution of this Proposal, will prevent too great a Reduction of the Interest of Money; because the continual inclosing and improving so much waste Land, as will be needful for the Purposes laid down in this Essay, will not only make abundance of Estates to be purchased, which are now not worth one fourth, perhaps, of what they will be when improved, but will raise such vast Quantities of Produce, and consequently Manu- 106 factures, to invest that Money in, which the Go- || vernment may from Time to Time be paying off; which Money, if this Way be not provided for employing and investing it, must again come to Market to find Interest; whereby the Plenty of Money, seeking Interest, will be so great, that Interest must sink, or, which is equivalent, the Premiums on Money at Interest advance, in such Proportion as the Plenty of Money seeking Interest shall increase; which Premiums, with the Interest thereof, must in the End be lost, in consideration of receiving three or four *per Cent.* for a Time, instead of such Interest, as the Plenty of Money seeking Interest would naturally bear.

But the executing this Proposal is absolutely need ful, as it is the only Means, whereby the Price of all Things can be lowered in such Proportion as the publick Securities shall be paid off: For these having now the Operation of Money, keep up the Price of all Things in Proportion to their Quantity, which, as they shall from Time to Time be paid off and annihilated, will be found to have just the same Effect in lowering the Price of every thing, as as if the Nation had really lost so much Gold and Silver. And though I think this self-evident, yet I shall quote *E. Phillips*, Esq; to support me, who, Page 42, says, there can be no doubt, that in the Year 1750, or thereabouts, when we may suppose the whole national debts paid off, and all the Paper Effects, which now have the Operation of Money, annihilated, all Goods will fall in their Price; because these Paper Effects being then sunk, their Operation must cease of Course. For as the Value of Commodities has || risen, by the Increase of Gold 107 and Silver within these 150 Years, so would they of Necessity fall in their Price, if our Gold and Silver were considerably diminished; the Consequence must be the same, if there is a Diminution of that which hath the Operation of Money.

'Tis true, as he further says, That as the Taxes will be abated, as the national Debts are paid off, so the Prices of Goods will fall in Proportion to the Abatement of the Impost on them; yet this will by no means suffer the Prices of Things to fall in Proportion to the sinking such a prodigious Value of Paper Effects, as at present operate with the full Force of Money amongst us; for these being several Times as great as our real Specie, must, by the aforesaid Rule, when sunk, make all Things fall in such Proportion, unless our real Specie can be augmented in the Interim to prevent it; and this, I doubt not, but it certainly will, if the Way I have pointed out, be heartily and sufficiently persued.

11*thly*, The full and sufficient Execution of this Proposal, will enable the Government to reduce the national Debts, and ease the Taxes.

For as the Produce of the Earth, and Consumption thereof, will certainly be greatly encreased, which Things always go together, the Revenue must, I think, increase too; since the Malt Tax, Excise on Beer, Duty on Leather and Tallow, and whatever other Parts of the Produce are taxed, would evidently be as much augmented as the Produce and Consumption of these would be augmented; and if at the same time the Circumstances of the People will 108 be generally a || mended, as I hope I have sufficiently made out; as they will thereby be better able to pay these and all other Taxes, so every thing being by the full and sufficient Execution of this Proposal made considerably cheaper, which will as certainly attend the Execution thereof, it's plain, the Government will be able to effect every thing with as much less Money as the Price of Labour and Goods of all Kinds will hence be reduced, and therefore will certainly have a Surplus of Revenue arising not only by the Augmentation thereof, but by being enabled to effect every thing, that they may have Occasion to do, with much less Sums than they can now effect those Things; and sure this Difference, which will certainly be very considerable, if sufficiently pursued, may be applied to reduce the national Debts, and ease the Taxes.

But perhaps it will be objected; that to effect this Proposal, the Land-tax will lessen with the Rents of Lands, whence the Revenue must in this Branch of it diminish. I answer; that most of the Counties are able, with ⅔ of the Tax on Land, to raise the Quota's assess'd on them. And *Eras. Phillips*, Esq; p. 44, supposes all the Lands in the Kingdom not to be assess'd at above half their Value; and if so, their Quotas, notwithstanding the Fall of Rents, may be still kept up; but if we add the Land-tax, that may be further raised on so great an Addition of Land, as must every Year be further put into Use and cultivated, to hold the needful Proportion to the natural Increase of Mankind, and effect the Things I am contending for; this Addition of the Land-tax will, undoubtedly, con || tribute so much to 109 the preventing any Diminution of this Branch of the Revenue, that, I think, we need have no Apprehensions about this Matter.   And if the People will encrease as Trade is relieved and enlarged, which is a Truth known even to a Maxim, there can be no doubt that the Revenue will certainly, in the whole, soon be augmented, and also in this Branch of it.

But because the Land, that shall be further put to Use, will be more in Proportion in some Counties than others, perhaps this may make a new Assessment of the Land-tax needful; which therefore in such Case should be done.

I can't dismiss this Head without shewing, that if all the Taxes were taken off Goods, and levied on Lands and Houses only, the Gentlemen would have more nett Rent left out of their Estates, than they have now the Taxes are almost wholly levied on Goods.

The national Debt is supposed to be near 50 Millions; the Interest of which, at 4 *per Cent.* is two Millions: And I further suppose, two Millions more may be near as much as is raised for the current Service of the Year, in these times of Peace; this together makes four Millions *per Annum*, which must be raised nett for the Government.

The Rental of the Kingdom, though it's at present assess'd but at 10, is well known to be 20 Millions *per Annum**; so that if the Land were fully assess'd

* *E. Phillips*, Page 44, says, I believe I shall be allowed to compute the Rents of the Kingdom at 20 Millions.

(as it certainly ought if it can be proved that the Land must pay all the Taxes, however the Manner
110 of collecting them ‖ be varied) four Shillings in the Pound would raise the whole Supply of four Millions, except the Charge of collecting it, which by Way of Land-tax being found to be but about 6 Pence in the Pound, or 2½ *per Cent.* will make but 100,000 *l.* more.

But let us see what it will cost the Nation to raise four Millions *per Annum* on Goods.

I suppose we have hardly less than 15,000 Persons employed, in the Kingdom, and upon the Coasts thereof, to collect, manage, and look after the Revenue in every Respect, besides a considerable Number of Vessels; the Charge of which, and Salaries of all these Officers of every Class, together with the Perquisites they receive from the People, which affect the Price of Goods just as if it were all nett Duty paid into the Treasury; all these Charges taken together, I suppose, may very moderately be reckoned equal to 100 *l. per Annum,* at a Medium, for each of those Persons. So that the Nation is thus necessarily put to a Million and an half Charge by these Officers; and if we suppose the Duties on Goods, and the Charge of collecting them, to be equal to ⅛ of the gross Value of them, then the gross Value will at this Rate be 33 Millions. Now since those that disburse the Duties, and Charge of collecting them, must have a suitable Profit to every Hand through which the Goods pass to the Consumers, I will suppose these Profits to inhance the Value of the Goods to the Consumers 8 *per Cent**.

---

* All Taxes on Commodities of universal Consumption raise, at least, 10 *per Cent.* more than their Rate on the People, because the Dealers in those Commodities exact that Interest for the Money advanced for the Tax: If I put this Exceeding at 15 *per Cent.* I believe Experience will justify me. See *Fog's* Journal of *February* the 20th, 1732 3.

this will occasion a further Charge to the ∥ Nation ₁₁₁
of 2,640,000 *l. per Annum.* So that collecting four
Millions for the Government on Goods, puts the
Nation to above four Millions more Charge, than
would be sufficient to raise the same Supply by way
of Land-tax only. And I verily believe, I have not
exceeded in any of my Suppositions; or if I have,
I doubt not that I am still in the whole Charge
enough within Compass, and that this Way of
Reasoning is just.

But before I proceed to shew that this whole
Charge of 8 Millions, which is equal to 8 Shillings
in the Pound on the Rental of the Kingdom, will all
fall ultimately on the Land, it is needful to shew
that the Land gives all we have.

That the Land gives all we have, would be self-
evident, if we did not import many Goods which are
the Produce of other Nations: But this makes no
Alteration in the Case; since the Quantity of foreign
Goods we import, can't continually be of greater
Value than the Goods we export, because this, in
the End, must exhaust all our Cash, and so put an
End to that Excess. Therefore the Goods we
import stand only in Place, and in Stead of those
we export; consequently the Land gives not only
all we have of our own Produce, &c. but virtually
all we re ∥ ceive from other Nations; since it pro- ₁₁₂
duces and delivers, at least, a Quantity equal in
Value to the Quantity of Goods we import. And
as I have now proved that the Land gives all we
have, notwithstanding the Importation of any Quantity of foreign Goods, I will next shew that it must

---

If we consider that Taxes on Goods inhance the Charge of Living, and
consequently of Labour, in some Degree at least, we can't doubt but that
the Taxes on Goods must inhance their Price to the Consumer, at least
as much as I have supposed, because Labour enters so essentially into
every thing, as to constitute the chief Value thereof.

pay all the Taxes, levy them how we will. I might, without going any further, insist on it, as a self-evident Principle, that that which gives all must pay all; but I will shew how this comes to pass in this Case. It hath been laid down as a certain Principle, That the Price of Goods to the Consumers in general, depends on, and is governed by, and will always be more or less, according as the Quantity of Cash circulating amongst the People is more or less, in Proportion to their Numbers.

And as the Rents of Lands depend also on this Principle, I will shew what the Rents of Lands will be in Consequence thereof.

Now the Rents of Lands can be no greater (nay they ought not to be so great) than the Overplus which remains to the Farmers, after all Charges, together with their own Subsistence, are deducted out of the Price or Sum, the Produce of the Land they rent fetches at Market; and Experience shews, the Rents of Lands will always be very near as much as this, since the Farmers in general, as well as every body else, find it as much as they can well do to pay their Rents. But to proceed.

Suppose the Cash, amongst the People in general, to be what it now is; and that all the Taxes were taken off Goods; it's evident, this would not, in the End, lower the Price of || Goods to the Consumers; since that Price, by the Principle laid down, depends on the Quantity of Money circulating amongst the People: But if the Duties were taken off Goods, they must cost as much less than they do now, as the Taxes now on them, with the Charges of collecting, &c. now inhance them; therefore, I think, if the Taxes were taken off Goods, and laid on Lands and Houses only, so much more Money must in this Case come to the Hands of the Farmers for the

Produce of the Ground, as would enable them to
pay as much larger Rents than they now can do,
as would double the Land-tax, if the whole Supply
were raised this Way only: and this I conclude
must be so, because the Charge of collecting the
Duties on Goods is, as hath been shewn, about
equal to the nett Supply for the Government, whilst
the Charge of collecting the Supply by Way of
Land-tax, doth not exceed $\frac{1}{10}$ Part of the Charge
of collecting it on Goods, as hath also been shewn.

But that I may make it evident that the Taxes,
and all Charges which attend collecting them on
Goods, must lessen the Rents as much as they
amount to, I reason thus: The Produce of the
Ground, when fitted for the Consumer, fetches a
certain Sum of Money, out of which all Charges,
from the raising it out of the Earth to the fitting it
for the Consumer, must be deducted, together with
the Taxes, and all Charges they occasion by collecting them; and the Overplus, after these are all
deducted, is all the Rent that can possibly be paid. ‖ 114

Now if the Taxes, and Charges they occasion in
collecting them on Goods, be equal to 7, 8, or 9
Shillings in the Pound on the Rental of the Kingdom, these, which deduct so much out of the Price
which the Goods fetch of the Consumers, must
deduct it ultimately out of the Rent. And if every
thing will always find its true Value, which is a
known Maxim in Trade, Land, which is most valuable of all Things, because it gives all Things, must
do so; therefore if the Taxes were all taken off
Goods, the Land would necessarily bear as much
higher Rents, as the Taxes substract from the Price
of the Goods it produces; and this will clearly appear, by shewing in what Manner taking the Taxes
off Goods will operate, to bring the whole Amount
of them into the Landlords Pockets for Rent.

If the Taxes were taken off Goods, they would come cheaper, and Cheapness would increase the Consumption, as Cheapness of every thing always doth; and that Increase of the Consumption would increase the Demand for those Things. Now since every thing is the Produce of the Ground, the Demand for the Produce would increase the Demand for Land, and that would necessarily raise the Rent, even till all the Money now paid for Taxes, together with all the Charge they are necessarily attended with, would come into the Landlords Pockets for Rent. Thus if the Taxes were taken off Goods, the Landlords would receive 8 or 9 Shillings in the Pound more Rent than they now do, if the Taxes on Goods do any way amount to so much; and if 4 Shillings in the || Pound or thereabouts would, as hath been shewn, raise the whole Supply for the Government, the Landlords would receive more Rent, by 4 Shillings in the Pound on their whole Estates, after the Taxes are deducted, than they can do whilst the Supply for the Government is raised on Goods.

Nor can this possibly be otherwise, unless the Money circulating amongst the People be not sufficient to augment the Rents so much: And though I allow it is not, yet I verily believe, if all the Taxes were taken off Goods, the Money we have would be found sufficient to augment the Rents, equal to the Taxes that would be needful to be laid on them; or, at least, that it would prevent any considerable Fall of the present Rents of Lands in general, even though so much Land were to be added and improved, as would be needful to answer the Purposes I am persuing in this Essay.

But perhaps it will be asked, if taking the Taxes off Goods will not in the End lower their Prices to the Consumers; as it certainly will not, because the Prices of all Commodities in general do necessarily depend on the Quantity of Money circulating amongst the People: I say, perhaps it will be asked, what Advantage the taking the Taxes off Goods will be to Trade? I answer, *First,* That all the Hands now employed in raising the Taxes on Goods, would be gained to contribute their Quota of Skill and Labour to encrease the publick Stock, who now, by living on the Publick, eat up so much of it as their whole Maintenance and Support amounts to, and thereby are at least a double || Loss to the Nation 116 of so much. And next, I say, that the Advantages that will arise to Trade by taking the Taxes off Goods, must be measured by the Inconveniencies which the Taxes on Goods occasion to Trade; and as these are felt by all to be prodigiously great, so the Advantages which will arise to Trade by taking the Taxes off Goods, must be found by all to be prodigiously great too, since they are Opposites that just equal each other.

And perhaps it may be asked, how the Price of Goods can be so strictly governed by the Quantity of Money circulating amongst the People, since the Prices of them frequently vary very much? I answer, that though the Seasons, and other Circumstances will indeed always vary the Prices of all Sorts of Things, yet it must be allowed that the Rise of Goods will necessarily lessen the Consumption of them, and that the Cheapness of Goods will so much augment the Consumption of them, as in the Event to make the Effect the same, as if they were strictly and invariably governed by the Quantity of Money circulating amongst the People.

And perhaps it will be objected; that if all the Duties were taken off Goods, Goods imported

8

would, in this Respect, have Preference to our own Goods, which in the End must pay both Rent and Taxes; but foreign Goods would in this Case pay neither.

In answer to which, I say; that since we must deliver Goods of our own Produce, equal in Value at least to those we import, as hath been shewn, the Goods we import should be deemed to have 117 paid Rent and Taxes, since they ‖ stand only in lieu of others of equal Value, which have paid both.

I am induced to treat on this Way of raising the Taxes rather than on Goods, because it may seem difficult, if not impossible, to get Hands enough to go into Tillage, &c. to carry this Proposal to its Perfection; and also because I have before shewn, that Trade, Manufactures, &c. will probably not be able to spare so many Hands, since the Demand for them will certainly cause better Wages to be given to Artificers, and Manufacturers, &c. than Plowing and Sowing will ever do: For Plowing, and Sowing, &c. reduce the Rates of Labour; but a Demand for Artists in the Manufactures always raises the Rates of Wages; therefore these will always, of themselves, draw the working People to them, if they are wanted.

And hence I conclude it needful, in order to carry this Proposal as far towards the End proposed, as the Nature of Things will admit, that the Taxes should be as gradually taken off Goods, and all the Officers in the publick Revenue, as gradually discharged, as this Proposal can be executed; that they may get their Livelihood in such a Way as will increase the publick Stock of Plenty, and that we may have none to succeed to live on the Labour of

the Industrious, as Multitudes always must*, as
long as any Taxes are raised on Goods. ‖   118

This Reasoning holds as to our Laws; which are
multiplied almost to Immensity, but ought to be
reduced to so small a Volume, and be so clear and
easy, that the meanest Subject may know the Laws
of his Country as well as the greatest.   This is the
Case in *Denmark*, and might be the same here;
and then a vast Number of Hands would be gained
to contribute to the Good of Society, in a Way
congruous to the Circumstances of Mankind.

And as to the Practitioners in Physick, I am sure
many of them must get their Livelihood this useful
Way, because most of the Diseases and Vices which
Mankind are so generally over-run with, will be
prevented: For Industry, and every social Virtue
will certainly take Place, and remove those Vices
and Corruptions, which have drawn in such prodigious Numbers, as this Profession is so horribly
surcharged with.

And many of those who (for want of this useful
Way to employ them) are now brought up to Divinity,
would soon find the Way to be more usefully em-

* In a Mass of People, there is not above one half labouring or manufacturing. For suppose we have 8 Millions of People, and that the Limits
of the Age of Labour be placed between 13 and 63, and that ⅝ of the
People are between these Ages; from these we must deduct at least ⅜,
under the following Classes; Females, sequestrated from Labour by the
Condition of their Sex; the Idle, by Rank or Choice; Men of Professions;
such as vend the Manufactures of others, but add no real Value to them;
the Sick and Impotent. By this Computation, there only remains one half
labouring or manufacturing. I am persuaded I put the Number too high,
and that there are not above three Millions of working People. The Price
of Labour is raised in proportion to the Scarcity of Labourers; they being
somewhat like their Commodities, dear in Proportion to their Scarcity:
Any Number of labouring People sitting idle increaseth the Price of
Labour, double of the Proportion which that Number bears to the whole.
For Example: Suppose three Millions of labouring People, and 30,000
Men carrying Arms, or levying Taxes; 30.000 is one *per Cent.* on 3
Millions, and these living on the Labour of the rest makes another one
per Cent. in all two, or double of that Proportion. See *Fog's* Journal of
January 20th, 1732-3.

ployed for their own Comfort and Support, than
119 the Generality of that Pro || fession now are, or
ever can be, till such a Demand for their Skill and
Industry is produced, as the full and sufficient Execution of this Proposal alone can effect. For can it
be imagined, that if so much Business could be made
as I am aiming at, such a vast Number as now
follows this Profession, the Generality of whom are
not only insufficiently but scandalously rewarded,
would not prefer the Profit, which, in every Employ,
must be necessarily connected with such a Quantity
of Business, as leaves it doubtful whether Hands
sufficient can be found to perform and transact it?
    As to the Sword, I would have every Person in
the Kingdom trained to all the needful military
Exercises, in the utmost Perfection, and that from
their earliest Capacity to receive any such Instruc-
tions; which, I am sure, would as effectually preserve
us from the unjust Attacks of our Neighbours, as
any Body of mercenary Forces we can maintain
will ever do. And, I think, we should be less liable
to make any unjust Attacks on our Neighbours, in
this Case; since Men will not easily be induced to
leave their Families and Livelihoods, to carry War
and Destruction to those that have not made it
necessary. But War seems now a civil Game, to
divert Princes, and employ the numerous Troops
they keep in Arms; whilst it is become so general
a Practice to keep a standing Force, that they are
almost become necessary even to free Kingdoms
and States.
    But if, after all, it should be found true, that we
can't get Hands enough into Tillage, &c. to carry
120 this Proposal compleatly to the End I || am aiming
at, yet this must itself be a cogent Reason for carrying this Matter as far as may be; since it is infinitely

for the Happiness of Mankind, rather to want Hands to do all the Work that may arise, than to have such a vast Number of Hands to spare, as are now degenerated into Vagabonds, relieved by the Publick, or almost perishing for want of Work enough to render Labour so valuable, as to be a sufficient, fit and natural Motive to make them industrious.

But, besides this Difficulty of wanting Hands sufficient to execute this Proposal effectually, 'tis objected, that the working People will not now work above 3 or 4 Days in a Week, but get drunk the other 2 or 3 Days; and that this would be worse, if Necessaries were rendered so cheap as I am contending for. In answer to which I must observe, that Necessaries can't be rendered so cheap, as I am aiming at, without employing more of the labouring Peoples Time and Labour, to raise such a Plenty of them as may make them cheaper. Nor can there be this additional Employment for their Time and Labour, till the Reduction of the Price of Necessaries shall not only be this Way attempted, but proceeded in: If therefore I can prove that, notwithstanding the working People do waste a great deal of their Time, they nevertheless do Work enough, and too much too, as Things now stand; and that they would do more, if it were provided in a Way that would encourage their Industry; I hope no such Stress ought to be laid on this Objection, as to hinder the Execution of this Proposal. ||　　　　　　　121

And, *First*, I say the working People do work enough; because there is always such a Plenty of all Kinds of Goods in the Hands of the Venders, that the Consumers can always buy what they want. This being undeniably true, shews that the working People, who alone make all these, do Work enough; the End of making them being to supply the Wants of the Consumers.

Again, I say, if it is become a Custom to hawk
Goods about, to such an extraordinary Degree,
that the Traders and Shopkeepers in most Parts of
the Kingdom have petition'd the Parliament to have
it prevented, because it disabled many of them to
live, and pay their Rents, as they justly alledge;
then there is not only Work enough, but too much
done; since it hurts both the Traders, and Landlords of Houses, by a greater Plenty of Goods than
those who should be the Consumers of them are
able to purchase: For this too great Plenty of Goods
is the sole Foundation of Hawking them.

The like may be said of giving any considerable
Credit, either as to Sums or Time. I wish I could
say, the Plenty of the Necessaries of Life was as
great as the Plenty of all other Things always is:
But this is so far otherwise, that but 4 or 5 Years
ago, many Thousands of Poor, in several Parts of
the Kingdom, were forced to live on such unwhol-
some Trash, as introduced a Distemper little less
than Pestilential, and almost, if not altogether as
fatal to them; whole Families being frequently
swept away by it in a few Days, and probably
122 many ‖ were actually starved to Death. See Mr.
Richard Bradley's Philosophical Enquiry into the
late severe Winter, and Scarcity and Dearness of
Provision.[18]

Again, if there be any flagrant Marks of a Decay
of Trade upon us (and I will presently produce
enough of them) then there is evidently more Work
done, than either our domestick or foreign Trade
doth require, let the Time wasted by our working
People be what it will: For a Decay of Trade, and
a sufficient Demand for the Goods we make, are
incompatible Things.

But I shall offer an Instance, to shew that the

working People can and will do a great deal more
Work than they do, if they were sufficiently encouraged. For I take it for a Maxim, that the
People of no Class will ever want Industry, if they
don't want Encouragement: The Truth of which is
as certain and undeniable, as that the Consumer,
if he had Money to pay for it, and was willing to
buy, never yet went entirely without any staple
Commodity whatsoever, or indeed without any other
common Thing he wanted. And if the labouring
People do so much Work under the discouraging
Wages, which I have shewn, are not equal to ⅔ of
the necessary Charge of a middling Family; what
might we not expect, if they were animated by a
sufficient Supply, and those Temptations removed,
which I have shewn, are the greatest Snares to them,
and which I think would certainly in a great Measure
be remov'd, if this Proposal were to be executed? ‖ 123

The Instance I shall produce, to prove that the
working People can and will do a great deal more
Work than they do, if they were somewhat better
incouraged, shall be that of a general Mourning for
the Death of a Prince.

The Charge brought against the working People,
as above, shews that they don't want Time to do
a great deal more Work than they do; and a Time
of general Mourning for a Prince necessarily requires abundance of Goods to be made in a very
short Time, besides the considerable Stock we may
suppose to be in Hand, towards supplying the extraordinary Demand of such Occasions; and we know
the Weavers, Dyers, Taylors, &c. do at such Times
work almost Night and Day, only for the Encouragement of somewhat better Pay and Wages, which an
extraordinary Demand for any Goods is necessarily
connected with; and if this can be carried so far,

as to cloath so great a Part of the People of the
Kingdom in so short a Time, as we usually see them
put themselves in Mourning on such Occasions, it
must be plain that the working People not only can,
but would do a great deal more Work than they do,
if they were but somewhat better encouraged by
their Wages to do so.

Lastly, The full and sufficient Execution of this
Proposal is the only natural Way to extend Dominion, and introduce Liberty amongst Mankind.
For wherever so much Land is continually put to
use, as will call for all the Hands, Trade, and Manufactures will suffer to employ themselves this Way,
as this will necessarily give full Employment to all
124 the People, and || make such Plenty of every Thing,
that the meanest of the People will certainly find a
comfortable Subsistence for themselves and Families, so it will infallibly draw the People out of
every Nation round us, that doth not attend to this
Point in the same Degree; and consequently cause
the People to forsake every arbitrary and oppressive
Government, to find such a Settlement, as the Business so much Land continually added and improv'd
will necessarily provide for them.

'Tis true, this will in Time fill this Island with
Inhabitants, and improve every Spot of Ground in
it. And I suppose it must be this Way that *Benjamin Motte* computes that the People may be doubled,
in so short a Time as 24 or 25 Years: If this be not
the Way, I am not able to conjecture how so great
an Increase of People should arise, in the small
Space he asserts they may be doubled and quadrupled; for I am sure the natural Increase of Mankind
will require a vastly longer Term, only to double in.

But however, if my 9th and 10th Principles are
true, and I think them self-evident, then the full and

sufficient Execution of this Proposal must be a great
Advantage to the Government, by increasing the
Number and Riches of their Subjects, and their
Revenues together with them, which Things are
inseparably connected.   Nay, this Matter ought
most certainly to be carried so far as to fill *Ireland*
with Inhabitants, by granting for a considerable
Term, on small Acknowledgments, a proper Quantity of any waste Land, that any Person shall choose,
and be able to ‖ undertake the full Improvement of. 125
And thus, I think, these Kingdoms would soon become vastly more powerful; since 'tis probable,
that in less than a Century there would be double
the present Number of People found in them.   Nor
could this possibly fail, I think, unless the Nations
round us, to prevent the Loss of their Subjects,
should take the same Measures; and then the Increase of each Nation would be only such as the
natural Increase of Mankind will produce.   But this
great Advantage would arise to Mankind by this
Means, that Happiness and Liberty would be as
general and extensive, as the Method I prescribe
shall be practised.

And this may shew the Folly and Absurdity of
making War, on the ambitious Principle of extending
Dominion; since War, if it be continued a few Years,
commonly ruins the Generality of the People of such
Nations as are vanquish'd; as we know the late War
did *France*; and what we who conquer'd got by it,
the Taxes we at present groan under, and from
which perhaps we shall never be reliev'd, will amply
testify.   But the Folly of making War, to extend
Dominion, appears, in that War lays waste and de-
populates Countries, and thereby puts such Nations
to great and extraordinary Charges and Difficulties,
to preserve and defend such unpeopled Territories

from the easy Inroads and Invasions of their Neighbours, who have as many more Oportunities of
Entrance, as the extended unpeopled Territory of
any Potentate doth necessarily afford.

    If therefore it be absurd to make War to extend
126 Dominion; I should rather say Terri ‖ tory, for that
is all that can be got by it*; and if, as I have before
shewn, it be unnecessary on the Account of Trade
also; it will follow that War, except in our own
necessary Self-defence, is unnatural and wicked;
since these ordinary Causes, *viz.* extending Dominion
or Trade will not justify it.

    Yet I think there is one Case, in which making
War on other Nations may be justifiable, *viz.*
Fighting for Territory when we are over-peopled,
and want Land for them, which our Neighbours
have, but will not part with on amicable and reasonable Terms. And as this, and necessary Self-
defence is all the just Foundation War can ever
have; so War for any other Cause is Murder,
aggravated by the horrible Addition of all the
Thousands that are destroy'd on both Sides. This
must be so, because it's monstrous to imagine, the
Author of the World hath constituted Things so,
as to make it any Ways necessary for Mankind to
murder and destroy each other: And yet he must
have constituted Things thus monstrously, if War
be necessary on any other Foundation whatsoever.

    I will now proceed to shew, that the State of the
Nation, in Respect of the Trade thereof, is really
very different, and much worse than it was about
the Year 1688.

    Erasmus Phillips says, *Page* 15, that the Year
above mentioned was perhaps the Time, when
England was in Possession of the greatest Quantity

---

* See the last Paragraph of the Spectator, No. 200.

of Wealth she ever did enjoy: She was then inrich'd
with the Treasure she had ‖ been accumulating for [127]
about 150 Years; for so long we may date the
Progress of Trade in this Nation. And *Page* 17,
he says, As to the Specie of the Nation, the Re-
coining 3 Years afterwards makes that Sum almost
apparent as to the Silver; for from 1691 to 1697,
there was brought to the *London* and Country Mints,
8,400,000 *l.* of clipt, light, and hammer'd Money,
and in all Probability there might be a great Sum
standing out. The mill'd Silver coin'd in King
Charles IId, and King *James* IId's Reign, might be
2,200,000 *l.* so that we may suppose subsisting in
Silver Money, at that Time, about 11 Millions.
And the Gold we may reckon thus:

Coin'd in Queen *Elizabeth*'s Time, who reform'd most of the old Specie	*L.* 1,500,000
Coin'd in King *James* Ist's Time	800,000
Coin'd in King *Charles* Ist's Time	1,723,456
And in the Reigns of King *Charles* IId, and King *James* IId.	6,500,000
In all	*L.* 10,523,456
But allowing for Deficiencies and Wastes of all Kinds	3,000,000
The Gold Specie then remains	*L.* 7,523,456
Silver Specie as above	11,000,000
Total of the Specie circulating in the Nation about the Year 1688.	*L.* 18,523,456

And *Page* 18, he says, There is Reason to believe
this was the State of the Nation in Respect to Trade
and Money in the Year 1688. ‖   [128]

And I will endeavour to shew, that the Trade of
the Nation had really stood on such a Foot, during
the whole Period of the Coinage above set forth,

that it was not likely we had thereby diminished any Part of the Specie abovemention'd, on which however so large a Sum as 3 Millions is allow'd for Deficiencies and Waste.

In the Year 1645 there were 7966 Christen'd, and 11479 Buried.

In the Year 1689 there were 14777 Christen'd, and 23502 Buried.

The Christenings and Burials, then, being at the Year 1689, about double the Number they were at the Year 1645, makes it evident that the People in *London* and *Westminster*, &c. within the Bills of Mortality, were doubled in about 44 Years, notwithstanding that great Plague which happened in this Period. And Dr. *Nichols* hath assured us, that the Country increased in the same Time, though not in the like, yet in a considerable Proportion.

Now since the Prices of all Things in general were as high, if not higher, when the People were so much increased, than the Prices of the same Things in general were when the Number of the People were so much less (and this I shall take for granted as a Thing sufficiently known;) therefore, since we had at the Year 1688 no considerable national Debts, or Paper Effects operating as Money, and thereby inhancing the Prices of Things above the Rates which the Specie itself would support them at, as every Thing which hath the Operation of Money, 129 though it be not such, will ‖ never fail to do ; I say, this could be only the Effect of a vast Increase of real Specie circulating, which thus supported, if not raised the Prices of Things amongst such a vastly greater Number of People, as there was in *London*, *&c.* and in the Kingdom in general, at or about the Year 1688, above the Number there was about 44 Years before.

And since we (having no Mines) could only have such an Increase of Specie arise, by the Balance of Trade being so mightily in our Favour, as to increase the Money so vastly in so short a Time as about 44 Years; I think there can be no room to imagine, the Specie, coin'd as above, was at all lessen'd in this Period.

But it will still be a Question, Whether the Specie was not diminish'd before the Year 1645; since the Beginning of the Coinage goes much further back. To which I answer, that it is well known that our Trade at 1645 was but of about 100 Years Date, and therefore I shall say it was but in its Youth. And as it is a Circumstance, always attending the Beginnings of foreign Trade in every Nation, to have the Balance in their Favour; because such Nations having no Mines, cannot have much Money amongst them,* on which Account ‖ their Produce 130 and Manufactures must needs be low in their Price: And as this is the chief, if not the only Circumstance which lays the Foundation of the Exportation of the Commodities of any Country; so this being then our Case, must needs be the Means of increasing the Gold and Silver amongst us, from the Time of Reforming the old Specie by Queen *Elizabeth*, to the Time whence I begin that great Increase of the People.   But further to establish this Point, give me Leave again to make use of Dr. *Nichols*'s Authority in the beforecited Place, where he says, "To con-"sider further how mightily this Nation of ours hath

---

* The Sum coin'd in Queen *Elizabeth*'s Time, who reform'd most of the old Specie, shews we then had not much Money amongst us; whereas the Sums coin'd in the Reigns of King *Charles* IId, and King *James* IId, being 6 Millions and an Half of Gold, and 2,200,000 in Silver, shew we had a vast Balance in our Favour, near 9 Millions being coin'd during these two Reigns.   And this suggests that my Argument is just, that asserts the vast Increase of People during these Reigns, was owing to such a vast Balance of Trade in our Favour.

"increased within a Century or two, notwithstanding
"the many civil and external Wars, and those vast
"Drains of People that have been made into our
"Plantations since the Discovery of *America*." If
the Nation did really increase so mightily within a
Century or two, and it be an undeniable Fact that
the Prices of Things advanced too during that Time,
we must during that Time have had an Increase of
Money, in Proportion both to such an Increase of the
People and Prices of Things, as hath been before
reason'd on this Point. Therefore I think it appears
more than probable, that the Specie coin'd as above,
was not diminish'd, but really circulating amongst
us about the Year 1688.

Let us now see how different the State of the
Nation, and consequently the Trade thereof, now is
¹³¹ in this Respect. ||

The Cash of the Nation is by most People, so far as I can learn, esteem'd to be about 10 or 12 Millions. But *Erasmus Phillips* endeavours to shew that it is*   } *L.* 15,000,000

And in his Preface, he says, the National Debt is 53 Millions, a sixth Part of which, he says, Foreigners are generally supposed to have; which, allowing the Debt to be now somewhat lessen'd, can hardly be put lower than†   } *L.* 8,000,090

The Balance of Specie, which we may then call our own, will be   } *L.* 7,000,000

* Mr. *Richard Bradley*, Professor of Botany in the University of *Cambridge*, and Fellow of the Royal Society, in his Philosophical Inquiry into the late severe Winter, and Scarcity and Dearness of Provisions, printed 1729, Page 5 and 6, says, "It was generally computed that we "had in *England*, in the Year 1715, about 13 Millions Sterling Money;

That is 11 Millions and an Half less than we had about the Year 1688.

Now whether this great Diminution of our Specie be attributed chiefly to the vast Expence of King *William* and Queen *Anne*'s Wars, as || without 132 doubt it must in a great Degree; or that the Balance of Trade since that Time hath been against us, and contributed to this Diminution; it's evident the State of the Nation, being now so vastly different in respect of real Specie we can call our own, must have a malignant Influence on our Trade; whilst the Prices of most Commodities and Necessaries of Life, by the Operation of Paper-Effects, are maintain'd at higher Rates than those Things bore before the Year 1688.

Therefore I conclude, Since we have so much less Specie we can call our own, and such a vast Value of Paper-Effects operating as Money, and are indebted to Foreigners such a great Sum, the Interest of which they are continually drawing from us, besides a vast National Debt; that the State of Trade is as much worse than it was in the Year 1688, as the State of the Nation is so: For the Relation between these are such, if rightly consider'd, that they ought to be esteem'd as but one and the same Thing, notwithstanding we seem to distinguish them by different Names.

Another Point, whence I argue that the Trade of

"of which it was reckon'd there were about 11 Millions circulating: But "since the Year 1720, and from thence to 1724 or 1725, there were scarce "7 Millions supposed to circulate; which, he says, must necessarily hurt "the poorer Sort of People;" and I say, every other Sort in general with them, though not in the same Degree, perhaps because, we know, as the Proverb says, the weakest must go to the Wall.

† *Fog*'s Journal of *January* 20, 173⅜ says, the Interest due to Foreigners upon the Publick Funds, may be put at 400,000 *l. per Annum*: If so, we must owe them at least 10 Millions; for that Sum at 4 *per Cent.* comes to but 400,000 *l.* and if we reckon the Interest lower, the Principal must be greater in such Proportion.

this Nation is in a worse State than it was about the Year 1688, is the different Increase of the People since that Time to the Increase in the preceding 44 Years.

In the Year 1730, there were 17118 Christen'd, and 26761 Buried.

In 1689, (which I stopt at,) 14777 Christen'd, and 23502 Buried.

The Difference increased is, Christen'd 2341 and 133 Buried 3259, or about ⅙ Part of the ‖ Number of the Year 1689; which shews the Increase of the People since that Time to be about so much: Which being so far short of the preceding Period of 44 Years, shews that our Trade is in as much worse State, as the Increase is less in near the same Length of Time.

But the great Increase, in the before-mention'd 44 Years, will be partly ascribed to the great Number of *French* Refugees, that came and settled here in that Period. But I think they could not have found a Settlement with us, if our Trade had not been in a very flourishing State, without improving so much waste Land as their Numbers required, and thereby reducing the Prices of our Produce and Manufactures in such Proportion: Whereas it's certain no such Fall happen'd, and therefore it follows we had so much greater Exports of our Produce and Manufactures, as were equal to the Imployment so great an Addition of Hands did require to support them. And the great Quantity of Money coin'd in this Period of doubling, which was perhaps equal to all we had before circulating amongst us, shews that this was the Case, since nothing but so much greater Exports than Imports, could have brought us such a Balance of Gold and Silver, or have supported the Prices of Things.

This therefore shews, that the Increase or Decrease of the People in any Nation, depends more
on the Balance of Trade than on any other Consideration whatsoever. For where the Balance is
considerably in favour of any Nation, there the
People finding Employment do || always flow; and 134
contrarywise, if the Balance be considerably against
a Nation, the People must forsake it; a melancholy
Proof of which some of our Colonies do furnish,
many People of all Degrees, if we can rely on our
News-Papers, abandoning them. Nor can they ever
be recover'd but by their raising Corn and Cattle,
which includes almost every Thing, instead of their
Staple of Sugar, &c. which they find will not produce
enough of the Necessaries and Comforts of Life for
all the People. But if they were to raise these
necessary Things, and make them so plenty as to
inable them to Work full as cheap as the *French*,
who have now got the Staple of Sugars from them,
and thereby that Trade from this Nation; our Plantations would soon bring that Staple back again, or
at least come in for their Share in it, and all other
Branches of Trade which their Soil and Climate are
by Nature most adapted to.

And since I have digress'd so far about our Plantations, which I have done for their sakes, I must
say, I can't think it good Policy to carry our People
to them, whilst we have waste Land enough at home
to improve and employ them; since by carrying the
People away, we lose so many Consumers of our
Produce, &c. and Occupiers of Rooms, if not of
Houses; which necessarily brings a proportionable
Loss to the Revenue with it, besides the Charge of
transporting and settling them.

Instead of which, did we but cause the Trade of
our Colonies to be put on such a Foot as I am

9

pointing out, People enough would soon forsake
135 arbitrary and oppressive Governments, ‖ to find so
happy a Settlement, as such a State of Trade in our
Plantations would of itself produce, and is necessarily connected with. And this I am as certain of,
as that Mr. *Corbert* in his Answer to the *French*
King (*Guardian* No 52)[14] was certainly in the right,
when he told his Majesty, That the People will
never stay and starve in any Country, if they know
of any other where they can subsist themselves
comfortably.

Another Point, whence I argue the State of Trade
to be worse than it formerly was, is the great Number
of empty Houses, not only in the Suburbs and new
Buildings, but in the *Strand, Fleet-street, Ludgate-
hill, Cheapside,* and *Cornhil:* For I think Houses
shut up in *Cheapside* and *Cornhil*, are an unanswer-
able Proof of the bad State of Trade in this City ;
and I suppose, if the new Buildings were extended
further than they are like to be, *Cornhil* could hardly
be affected by them ; since so long as the *Royal-
Exchange* stands there, and Ships can't sail thro'
London-Bridge, it should, I think, be the Seat of
Trade, as it is certain it hath heretofore been. But
how is its State of Trade alter'd ! How many
Milliners, Pastry-Cooks, and other inconsiderable
Trades fill the Houses, where opulent wholesale
Dealers dwelt, whilst several other Houses have
been shut up for some Time ! And to me it appears
absurd, to impute this to any other Cause than the
different State of the Trade of this Metropolis *,

---

* That the Trade of this Metropolis is so much worse than it formerly
was, is ascribed to the Peace, which hath open'd the Trade of all the
Ports of the Kingdom, so that they can carry on Foreign Trade in most
of them, which during the War was chiefly carried on at this Port only,
the Trade of the other Ports not being considerable enough to obtain
Convoys, without which hardly any foreign Trade could be carried on in

which || I shall always regard as an Index of the 136 State of the Trade of the whole Kingdom.

I have before taken Notice, that the great Number of empty Houses is ascribed to the new Buildings of late Years. But I can't conceive the Buildings in the last forty Years, to have been near equal to what they must have been in the preceding forty Years, when the Buildings must have been so numerous as to equal the whole Number standing in *London*, *Westminster*, and the Suburbs thereof before that Time; because the People having doubled in the next forty Years (as appears by the Bills of Mortality) must needs have double the Habitations to reside in. And here I wave the Buildings which the Fire of *London* occasion'd, tho' that must have been prodigious, for it happen'd in this Period of doubling. Nay, it must be evident, the Buildings this last forty Years, can't have been near equal to the Buildings in the preceding forty Years, because abundance more Houses wou'd now be empty than there are, if this were the Case, since the People have not increased above ¼, or thereabouts, for the last forty Years, tho' they doubled in the preceding 40 Years, or thereabouts, as hath been shewn.

Another Point, whence I argue, that Trade is in a much worse state than it formerly || was, is that 137 we send Money to *Spain*, whence we ought most certainly to receive it: For *Spain* having the Mines of *Peru* and *Mexico*, and being so very careful to keep the Riches of them to themselves, that they search all Ships in those Parts, and if they find any Money on Board, confiscate them, and bring all the

War time. In answer to which, I shall only observe, that all the Ports in the Kingdom were as open and free to carry on foreign Trade, during most part of the Period in which it hath been shewn the People in *London*, *Westminster*, and Suburbs doubled, as those Ports have been since the *Utrecht* Peace.

Treasure of those Mines home to *Old Spain*, in the
King's Ships call'd *Galleons*, Register-Ships, *&c.*
Therefore *Spain* being the great Receiver of this
vast Treasure, consequently must have the Prices
of all Commodities at as much higher Rates than
other Nations, as the Wealth these Mines continually
furnish, is greater than any other Nation can receive,
who have no Mines but their Trade.

And as it is this which doth, and which in the very
Nature of the Thing should give us and other Nations, who have no Mines, the Advantage of vending
Goods to *Spain*, so as to have the Balance on them,
and every Country that hath Gold and Silver Mines;
so it will follow, that our Trade is really in a bad
Condition, if we pay them any Money at all. And
yet by our Bills of Entries it appears, that we Exported to *Cadiz* in *Spain*,

September 7, 1732	– –	2000 Ounces of *Gold*
9	– – – –	2000
Novemb. 4	– – – –	2000
Decemb. 16	– – – –	3000
19	– – – –	1000
January 7	– – – –	3000

138   In all 13000 Ounces of *Gold*,||

or about *L.* 50,000 in so short a Time. I could
produce many more Instances from the Bills of
Entry; but these are sufficient to prove that the
State of our Trade is not only worse than it formerly
was, when we undoubtedly had the Balance in our
favour on *Spain*, but that the Trade of this Nation
is in a very bad Way indeed; unless it can be proved
that Gold in *Spain*, is so much more valuable in
respect of Silver, than it is with us, that it will purchase so much more Silver in *Spain* than it will do
here, as is sufficient to pay the Freight of the Gold
out, and of the Silver home, and the Insurance for

the Hazard of the Sea out and home, with Postage of Letters, and Commission to the Merchants in *Spain*, and a Profit sufficient to induce our Merchants to export Gold to bring home Silver for it.

And besides all these Articles, together with the Interest of the Sums for the Time such a remote Voyage as *Cadiz* will require; for the Return can hardly be put at less than 5 *per Cent.* that Silver must be cheaper with respect to Gold in *Spain*, than it is with us; I think I may be positive that the Difference cannot be so great between these Commodities, since *Portugal*, which abounds in Gold from the *Brazils*, would find their Account in this Trade, which by their Neighbourhood with *Spain*, they cou'd carry on at half the Charge, and for half the Profits, which our great Distance from *Cadiz*, makes absolutely needful for us.

And since the Merchants in *Portugal* understand getting Money as well as others, can we imagine their Gold would come to us, as we || find by its Circulation amongst us it doth, if they could buy Silver with it at such cheaper Rates in *Spain*, as would enable them to send us Silver at so much higher Rates in respect of Gold, as the Silver would thus cost them less than it is worth with us, in respect of Gold?

Hence therefore I conclude, that nothing but *Spain*'s having such a Balance upon us, can be the Cause of our sending them this Money. And, I think, nothing but our Paper Effects, which are almost immense, if we consider the publick Securities of every Kind, and Bank Notes, *&c.* which have the Operation of Money amongst us, could possibly raise and keep our Markets so high, as to cause us to receive more Goods in Value from *Spain* than they take of us. And yet, I think, this must be our Case, tho' we carry them only Gold. And thus it may be said, we carry Coals to *Newcastle*; nor can the Event be different, if we go on so, except that this Matter is of so much more Importance, as Gold is more valuable than Coals.

I must own I have heard it supposed, that the Merchants in *Spain*, to avoid the Delays that of late Years have attended the Delivery of the Money from on Board the King's Ships, and also to elude paying the *Indulto* thereon, have found means to convey their Money by our Ships to *England*, and that this occasions the Exportation of Gold to *Spain*; but I think this Trade so dangerous, both to the Merchants in *Spain*, and our Ships too, that I know not how to admit this for a sufficient Reason.

Another Point, from whence I shall argue that 140 our Trade is in a much worse State than || it formerly was, shall be the following Estimate of the necessary Charge of a Family, in the middling Station of Life, consisting of a Man and his Wife, four Children and a Maid-Servant; so as I think a Person that hath such a Family, and employs *L.* 1000 of his own Money in Trade, ought to live. For if such Families must not have Necessaries enough, and I believe it will appear I have allow'd no Superfluities, I think we ought to give up Trade, and find some other way to live. For Trade terminates ultimately in the Consumption of Things, to which End alone Trade is carried on: Therefore if those that employ *L.* 1000 of their own Money, shall not be able to supply such a middling Family with needful and common Things, What then becomes of the Consumption of Things? or, in other Words, What becomes of Trade? For, to be sure, not one Person in a good many is the real Owner of such a Sum.

If therefore such Families must retrench and abridge themselves of common needful Things, those in Trade below them, in this respect, must 141 much more do so, if they have Families. ||

An Estimate of the necessary Charge of a Family in the middling Station of Life, consisting of a Man, his Wife, four Children and one Maid Servant, which I take to be a middling Family.

	per Head *per* Day	Daily Expence		Weekly Expence			Yearly Expence	
	d.	*s.*	*d.*	*l.*	*s.*	*d.*	*l.*	*s.*
Bread for seven Persons	¾		5¼		3	0¾		
Butter —— ——	¾		5¼		3	0¾		
Cheese —— ——	¼		1¾		1	0¼		
Fish and Flesh Meat ——	2½	1	5½		10	2½		
Roots and Herbs, Salt, Vinegar, Mustard, Pickles, Spices and Grocery, except Tea and Sugar	½		3½		2	0½		
Tea and Sugar ——	1		7		4	1		
Soap for the Family Occasions, and Washing all manner of Things both abroad and at home ——	1½		10½		6	1½		
Threads, Needles, Pins, Tapes, Worsteds, Bindings, and all sorts of Haberdashery ——	½		3½		2	0½		
Milk one Day with another ——			¾			5¼		
Candles about 2½ lb. *per* Week the Year round —— ——					1	3		
Sand, Fullers Earth, Whiting, Small Coal, Brick-dust ——						2		
10 Shilling Small Beer, a Firkin and a Quarter *per* Week ——					3	1½		
Ale for the Family and Friends					2	6		
Coals, between 4 and 5 Chaldron *per Annum* may be Estimated at ——					2	6		
Repairs of Houshold Goods, as Table Linnen, Bedding, Sheets, and every Utensil for Houshold Occasions ——					1	6		
6 *s.* 2 *d.* *per* Head Weekly for seven Persons amounts to near ——				L.2	3	1½	112	10 ‖ 142

	Yearly Expence	
	l.	s.
Brought over	112	10
Cloaths of all Kinds for the Master of the Family	16	
Shaving 7 s. 6 d. per Quarter, and cleaning Shoes 2 s. 6 d. per Quarter	2	
Cloaths for the Wife, who can't wear much, nor very fine Laces with	16	
Extraordinary Expence attending every Lying in L. 10, supposed to be about once in two Years	5	
Cloaths for four Children, at L. 7 per Ann. each Child	28	
Schooling for four Children, including every Charge thereunto relating, supposed to be equal at least to ten Shillings per Quarter for each Child	8	
The Maid's Wages may be	4	10
Pocket Expences for the Master of the Family, supposed to be about four Shillings per Week	10	8
For the Mistress of the Family, and for the four Children to buy Fruit and Toys, &c. at two Shillings per Week	5	4
Entertainments in return of such Favours from Friends and Relations	4	
Physick for the whole Family one Year with another, and the extraordinary Expence arising by Illness, may be much more than	6	
A Country Lodging sometimes for the Health and Recreation of the Family, or instead thereof, the extraordinary Charge of nursing a Child abroad, which in such a Family is often thought needful	8	
	L. 225	12
Rent and Taxes may be somewhat more or less than	50	
Expences of Trade with Customers, and travelling Charges, Christmas-Box-Money, and Postage of Letters, &c. for the sake of even Money, at least	19	8
Bad Debts which may easily be more than 2 per Cent. on the supposed Capital of L. 1000	20	
	L. 315	
There must be laid up, one Year with another, for twenty Years, in order to leave each Child, and a Widow if there should be one, L. 500	75	
L. 1000 therefore by this Estimate should gain one Year with another	390	‖

143

Which for the sake of a round Sum I will call 40 *per Cent. per Annum*, in order to support such a Family, and provide *L.* 500 a Piece for four Children, and a Widow, if there should be one left, which if not, will augment each Child's Share but *L.* 125. And here I suppose a Man to live twenty Years from his Marriage to his Demise, which I take to be about the Term one Man or Woman with another doth live. I don't mean by this that no Man or Woman lives longer from the Time of Marriage than twenty Years; I know many live much longer; but I am equally certain that as many never reach this Term as others live beyond it. And it will also many Times happen, that 5, 6, 7, 8 or more Children must be brought up by some Parents, tho' perhaps it will more frequently happen that less than four will be raised by others.

But those that shall happen to have seven or eight Children, will find the 75 *l. per Ann.* supposed in this Estimate to be laid up, in order to provide 500 *l.* a Piece for four Children, hardly sufficient to bear the extraordinary Charge, which so many more Children will occasion in this Rank of Living. And surely it must be very hard, that the Man who happens to have a numerous Family (and many such there always are) should thereby be render'd not only uncapable to provide any Thing for them to set out in the World with, but be reduced in a Course of Years, as he certainly must, if *L.* 1000 in Trade will not produce at least 40 *per Cent. per Annum.* ‖   144

But I have not produced this Estimate, only to shew what is the needful Charge for the decent Support of such a Family in this Rank of Life, but chiefly to shew that our Trade is in a much worse State than it was about forty or fifty Years ago:

For then it was a very common Thing for People,
from small Beginnings, to raise L. 5000 or more
for each Child, tho' the Families were as large as
my Estimate supposes: Which is a Truth so well
known, that I shall not attempt any Proofs of it,
but take it for granted, not doubting that the Observation of the aged and judicious Tradesman will
allow it me; and further concur, that the State of
Trade in general will now by no means admit of
making 40 *per Cent. per Ann.* on a Capital of L. 1000,
or perhaps hardly more than half as much.   Yet I
will not say there are no Instances of such Profits;
for perhaps such there will be, as long as there is
Trade amongst us: But I am certain they are few,
and hard to be found or guess'd at, there being too
many People in almost every Occupation to admit
of such Gains.   And I am as certain, that the Instances of raising pretty Fortunes for Children,
about forty or fifty Years ago, from very small Beginnings, were vastly more numerous than any are
to be found, at this Time, that can make any thing
near 40 *per Cent. per Ann.* on a Capital of L. 1000.
And therefore, I think, I may justly conclude, that
Trade is now in much worse Circumstances than it
formerly was.   But were our Trade to be put on
the Foot I am pointing out, less than 30 *per Cent.*
145 *per Annum* || on such a Capital, wou'd be as sufficient
for the Support and Provision of such a Family, as
40 *per Cent. per Ann.* is, as the Prices of Things
now go: And then the Demand for, and Consumption of every Thing would be so much augmented,
that it would be as easy to make 30 *per Cent. per Ann.*
on such a Capital, as it is now to make 20; for then
our Trade would be in that flourishing State I am
aiming at.

But from what I have now said, and also from this

Estimate, it must appear, that the Wealthy have
the Business and Affairs of the trading Part of the
People transacted, on Terms as much below the
reasonable and just Value thereof, as the Profits
such a Sum will generally make, are less than the
Estimate shews to be needful for a middling Family
in this Rank of Life. Therefore such diffusing
Property amongst the People in general, as hath
been before in this Essay represented, is absolutely
needful, not only for the Sake of the labouring
People, but for the trading Part too; who together
undoubtedly are more than 19 Parts in 20 of the
People of the Kingdom*; the Generality || of whom, 146
by the several Estimates, appear to be in equal
Difficulties, in Proportion to their Stations in Life.
And if so, is there any room to wonder at the Misery
we see amongst the Poor, or the Ruin which so
frequently befals the middling People; since by
both the Estimates it appears, the Nature of Things,
in our present Circumstances, is so big with these
Evils, that we may much rather wonder the Misery
and Ruin are not universal?

Again it must appear by this Estimate, that if
1000 *l.* employ'd in Trade, ought to make so large

* Let us see how many Gentlemen we may be supposed to have in the
Kingdom, by dividing the whole Rental of 20 Millions into *L.* 500 *per
Annum*, for each Gentleman, at a Medium; which I am sure is cutting
it into as many Pieces as it can be reasonably imagin'd there are Gentlemen that subsist solely on their Estates. Now 20 Millions divided by 500
gives 40,000, the Number of Gentlemen which, on this Supposition, live
on their Estates in this Kingdom: But if we consider how many large
Estates there are, and how few Gentlemen can subsist on *L.* 500 *per
Annum*, as the Prices of Things now go, it's very unlikely there are near
this Number of Gentlemen that subsist solely on their Estates. And yet
this Number, which, including their Families, with Servants and all,
I shall put at 8 Souls at a Medium, is but $\frac{1}{25}$ Part of 8 Millions of People,
which are supposed to be the least we have in the Kingdom. The rest
therefore, except such as have Places under the Government, must necessarily be subsisted by Trade or Labour; and their Number must, by this
Rule, be more than $\frac{19}{20}$ of all the People in the Kingdom, as I have
asserted above.

a Gain as about 40 *per Cent. per Ann.* all necessary
Means should be used, to make as large a Consumption of all Kinds of Goods, as the Nature of
Things is well capable of; which, as hath been
before sufficiently shewn, can hardly ever be equal
to what the Wants of the People, according to their
several Ranks and Stations only, will necessarily
require. And this should also be done, for the sake
of returning the Capitals employed in Trade, as
frequently as possible; since the quicker the Returns are made, the cheaper will the Goods come
to the Consumer; and the slower the Returns are
made, so much larger should the Profits always be,
that is, so much dearer ought the Goods to be sold
to the Consumer. If this is not the Case, the
147 Tradesman must suffer, ‖ which is very unreasonable, since all Trade is carried on solely for the Use
and Benefit of the Consumer.

Again, this Estimate shews, how unfit it is to give
or take long Credit in Trade; since the Advance
of the Price of Goods sold on Time, ought not to be
reckon'd with any Regard to the Interest of Money
on Securities, but by the Rates of the Profits which
the Capitals employ'd may require to answer the
End of Trade, which is not only the continual Support of Families, but such a Provision for them as
may, at least, leave the Children in Condition to fill
up the same, if not better Stations in Life, than their
Parents were in. For as all below this Point ap-
proach so much nearer Poverty, so, if such Descent
towards Poverty be too general amongst the trading
People, the Rents in general will not only fall, but
be lost; and this, I imagine, is both seen and felt
too at this Time.

And therefore, I think, giving long Credit in Trade,
which is now become much too general, ought to be

remedied; since it must affect the Landed-Men, either in the high Price of their Consumables, or in their Rents, or perhaps in both.

The last Thing I shall mention, to shew that our Trade really is, and hath been, for some considerable Time past, growing into a much worse State than it formerly was, shall be the acknowledged Dearness of the Labour of the People in *England*, to the Price of Labour in most of our Neighbour Nations; the Effect of which hath been so detrimental to our Trade, || that the Nations round us 148 have, in less than half a Century, enter'd on, and set up the Fabricating many Manufactures, which they before that Time had from us only: Which hath not only been observed, but lamented by many of our Merchants and Tradesmen, *&c.* And at length, as is notoriously known, the Dearness of Labour hath been found so burthensome to our Farmers, that the Gentry and Justices of the Peace, in their open Quarter Sessions, have lately, in several Places in the Kingdom, attempted to redress this Evil, by regulating the Rates of Servants Wages. Now this Attempt, though it be unnatural, and impossible to answer the End, is however a publick Acknowledgment, that our Trade is in a very bad State. For if our Labour be really too dear, as it most certainly is, then all our Commodities must be so too; which must necessarily greatly lessen the Vend and Consumption of them. And hence it will follow, that this publick Attempt to reduce the Rates of Labour, amounts to a publick Declaration that our Trade is in a very bad State.

But after all I have offer'd, which I think abundantly sufficient to prove that our Trade is in a much worse State than it formerly was, I know it will be objected, that we have, at this Time, as much

Trade amongst us in the Nation as we ever had; and that therefore our Trade is not so bad, as I have shewn it to be. Now, tho' I should allow the Objectors their Assertion, yet, I think, I can notwithstanding produce several Reasons, to shew that our Trade is in a much worse State than it formerly
149 was; as, ||

First, That the People in this Kingdom have increased considerably within the last half Century: For I have before shewn that this Town is increased about ¼ Part, in the Space of about forty Years. And Sir *William Pettis* says, A Nation will double itself in 200 Years, if it be free from War, Pestilence, or Draining for distant Colonies.[15] Now 40 Years being ⅕ of the Period he asserts a Nation will double in, it follows, by this Authority, that the People in this Kingdom must be increas'd ⅕ within the last forty Years: If therefore our Trade be not ⅕ Part greater than it was about forty Years ago, which I am sure cannot be shewn, it follows, that as our Trade is less, in Proportion to this Increase of People, than it formerly was, it therefore must be so much worse.

I am sensible it may be objected, that we have, within half a Century, had two Wars with *France*, as well as one in *Ireland* upon King *William*'s coming in; and that therefore this Authority will not support so great an Increase as I have deduced from it. But I answer, That we had so good a Trade about the Revolution, and during both those Wars with *France*, as drew more People from abroad to us, than these Wars did probably destroy.

Again, *Secondly*, allowing that we have now as much Trade in this Kingdom as we formerly had, yet it must also be allow'd, that if Trade be now carried on for less Profit, than it formerly was, as it undoubtedly is; and this I fear not will be generally granted; besides, that I think, what I have said under the last Estimate, doth sufficiently prove as much: I || say, if Trade be now carried on for less 150 Profits; and if the Charge of Living be likewise grown much greater than it formerly was, which I know will easily be allow'd me too, surely then Trade must necessarily be much worse than it formerly was, notwithstanding we may have as much Trade as we formerly had.   But altho' the Proofs I have given, are sufficient to shew that Trade is certainly in a much worse State than it formerly was, especially in this Metropolis, I think it will not be unnecessary to shew how Trade stands in the Country in this respect.

Now it hath been long asserted, that many Farmers, in several Parts of the Kingdom, from the Cheapness of the Produce of the Ground, and from the Dearness of Labour have been obliged to throw up their Farms to their Landlords.   And of late this is grown so generally the Case, that the News-Papers* have assured us, that most of the Farmers all over the Kingdom must inevitably have been ruin'd, had not Corn, &c. taken a sudden considerable and unexpected Rise, which the War now broke out in *Italy* hath occasion'd. And this seems to be allow'd to be Fact, even by the most sanguine of those that contend for the present most flourishing State of our Trade, whilst they content themselves with assigning this Cause for it, *viz.* That the Gentry truly do not now live, and spend their Money in the Country, as for || merly.   Now this, 151

---

* *Leghorn*, *Nov.* 7.   The Emperor hath strictly prohibited the Exportation of Corn from *Naples* and *Sicily*.——Whence we hope the Demand for *British* Corn in *Spain* and *Italy* will be so great, as to save our Farmers from the inevitable Ruin which must otherwise have attended them.   *London* and *Whitehall* Evening-Posts of *Nov.* 17, 1733.

if it be true, seems to me a very inadequate Cause, either of the late Cheapness of the Produce, or present Dearness of Labour; to which Causes the Farmers justly attribute the unhappy Dilemma they have for some Time labour'd under.

But however; Fact it seems it is, that the Farmers, generally, were so near inevitable Ruin as is above asserted: Now I would fain know what the State of Trade must be in the Country, when the Farmers in general were in so dreadful a Condition: For the Trade in the Country, I think, turns chiefly, if not entirely, upon the general Prosperity of the Farmers; for I believe the Country People would be able to raise but few Manufactures, if the Farmers in general were so reduced, as to be unable to raise the Principles out of the Ground, for them to work on; and yet this must be the Case, if the Farmers were generally ruin'd. For the Gentlemens employing their Farms themselves, would not mend the Matter; since they find by Experience, those Farms always bring them in Debt, on which the Farmers find they can't get a Livelihood; which therefore in the End, must ruin the Gentlemen as well as the Farmers. And therefore it follows, that, allowing the above Fact to be true, the Trade in the Country, as well as the Trade in *London*, is in a much worse Condition than it was formerly, when the Prosperity of the Farmers, and other Circumstances, enabled the Gentlemen almost universally to raise their Rents, as it's well known they have done very considerably, 152 within the Space of 30 or 40 Years last past. ||

But I shall now proceed to obviate an Objection, which, as Things are now circumstanced, may seem to lie against this Proposal, *viz*. 'Tis objected, that the Plenty is now so great, as to reduce the Price of the Produce so low, that the Farmers can pay no Rent; and therefore it follows, that we have already broke up and improv'd too much Land; since such Plenty can arise only from having too much Land in Use.

In answer to which, I shall first observe, that the Price of Things may be reduced too low to answer and turn to Account, not only from the Plenty of those Things consider'd in themselves, but from the Inability of the People in general to purchase them, in such Quantities as their Wants may require; since a considerable Abatement of the Consumption of any Thing, will operate to the Reduction of its Price, more than even Plenty of any Thing, consider'd with due Regard to the Wants of the People, will do*; and whoever considers the two Estimates I have produced, which shew ‖ how much greater 153 the Wants of the People are, than they can in general be supposed to get, must ascribe the present low Rates of the Produce, at least as much to an Abatement of the Consumption, as to the Plenty consider'd as aforesaid; since by those Estimates it plainly appears, the Wants of the People are mightily abridged.

Again, this Objection is contrary to the Nature of the Thing itself; since it suggests that Plenty is so enormous an Evil, as in general to ruin the

---

* If the Wants of the People are too much abridged, they must on that Account want Employment, and lose Time, which will make the rest of the Time they work more valuable, seeing they must have a whole Subsistence, tho' they shou'd be supposed to work but half their Time: Whence the Things they make will become too dear to answer, and turn to Account, because the Want of a sufficient Demand for, and Consumption of them, which are Consequences connected with these Circumstances, will at the same Time (that it inhances the Charge of making them) depress the Value of them. On the contrary, if we would make Things cheap, the People must, if possible, lose no Time; because only such full Employment can make every Thing cheap, and put it in the Power of the People to purchase, and consume all the Things they raise, and make. And hence only can the Demand become great enough, to make them answer, and turn to Account.

Farmers and Gentlemen. For if the Farmers can't
pay their Rent, they will certainly one time or other
be seized on, and torn to Pieces; and the Gentlemen
must also be ruin'd, if they can get no Rent for their
Lands, as this Objection suggests. Now since Plenty
is in its own Nature a general Good, and a universal
Blessing, always promoting and increasing the Consumption thereof, nor can possibly ever be otherwise; this Objection, which suggests that Plenty is
an Evil, and so great a one too, must be contrary
to the Nature of the Thing itself.

Again, if it were true, as this Objection suggests,
that we have already so much Land in Use, as makes
the Plenty so great, as to reduce the Price of the
Produce so low, that the Landlords can get no Rent
for the Lands; yet if it can be made appear (as I
think by what I have said in this Essay it doth) that
more Land is wanted to give full Employment to all
the People, and thereby to supply their reasonable
Wants, it will follow, whether Gentlemen can or
154 cannot get any Rent for their Lands, that the ||
People have a just and reasonable Right to have
so much more Land put to Use, as shall be needful
and sufficient to give them full Employment, and
subsist them comfortably; because every Person is,
by Nature, as much intitled to all the Land he can
cultivate and use, as he is to the Air in which he
breathes: For he can no more live without cultivating the Ground to supply his Wants, than he can
breathe without Air. And therefore, since Mankind
are all by Nature born equal in this respect, it can
never be reasonable to abridge any Part of Mankind
of this their natural Right, unless it can be clearly
prov'd, that it is for the Good of every Individual
to be thus abridged; and therefore, that they ought
either to purchase, or pay Rent for the Land they

shall use and enjoy. And this indeed, I doubt not,
I could clearly make appear, if I were to shew the
Preference of Civil Government, rightly administer'd,
to a simple State of Nature without Government;
of which the *Hottentots* seem to me to be the chief,
if not the only Instance we have now perhaps in the
World; and yet, I believe, I should prefer their
abject Condition to any arbitrary or oppressive
Government on Earth. But I deny that there is,
or ever was such a Plenty as this Objection suggests;
because the Produce of the Ground, when brought
to Market by the Farmers, is always sold for ready
Money. Now it is impossible that any Thing can
properly be said to be too plentiful, for which the
Demand is always so great, as to make it a ready
Money Commodity. For if the Plenty were really
too great for the De || mand, it would, as we know 155
many sorts of Goods and Manufactures are, necessarily be sold for Time. And since nothing but a
greater Plenty of any Thing, than the Demand for
it requires, is the Foundation and Cause of selling
such Things on Credit, it follows, that the Produce
is not too plentiful, since it's always sold for ready
Money. Nay, Victuals and Drink, which are the
only Things in this Objection I am properly concern'd with, are so far from being too plentiful, that
they are generally sold for ready Money, even down
to the meanest Consumer. For the Number of
those who do not 'pay present Money for these
immediate Necessaries, are not only few in Comparison, but even those Persons, generally speaking,
always pay for these immediate Necessaries in a
very short Time, unless when such a one happens
to be trusted, that is not able to pay at all. And
this, I believe, is so generally known to be true,
that I need not fear having the Concurrence of the

People in general on my side; by which the Truth
of this Argument must stand or fall, no other Proof
being possible in this Case.

If therefore it be not the Plenty of the Produce,
that is the Cause that it is at present sold so cheap,
that the Farmers can pay no Rent, as I think I have
sufficiently proved it is not, it will be necessarily
required to shew what is the Cause of so melancholy
a Truth, as this Objection is founded on. For I
allow that perhaps there never were so many Farms
quitted, and thrown on the Gentlemens Hands in
156 *England*, as at this Time. ||

Now this Cause I assert is chiefly, if not solely
owing to too great a Scarcity of Money amongst
the People in general. And in order to prove this,
I must shew what are the Signs of a sufficient Plenty,
and of too great a Scarcity of Money amongst the
People.

Now the Signs of a sufficient Plenty of Money
are these; the Houses well fill'd with Inhabitants,
the Rents well paid for them, and Fines exacted;
as also, that the Rents for Lands in general be well
and duly paid; and that we be not over-burthen'd
with Poor; nor our Roads or Streets infested with
Highwaymen and Robbers: When Things are thus
circumstanced, Trade may be truely said to be in a
flourishing State, or Money, on which Trade floats,
may be said to be sufficiently plentiful; and more
plentiful than this it never can be.

On the other hand, since it is now notorious that
the Number of empty Houses is very great, and
instead of Fines for them, as formerly, the Rents
are lower'd, and still falling; besides, that the Landlords very frequently fit them up too for the Tenants;
and our Poor are so very much increased, that we
are obliged to transport many of them; and our

Roads and Streets are so exceedingly infested with Highwaymen and Robbers, as perhaps the like was never; and since the Objection says, the Landlords can now hardly get any Rents for their Farms: These Signs therefore, being exactly the Reverse of the former, must needs be as certain and evident Proofs of a Decay of Trade, or, which is tantamount, of too great a Scarcity of Money amongst the People in general, ‖ as the aforemention'd Circumstances 157 were Signs and Proofs of a flourishing Trade, and a sufficient Plenty of Money amongst the People in general; nor do I know what Kinds of Proofs could be produced, or reasonably required besides, or stronger than these.

For if, when the Houses were well fill'd with Inhabitants, the Rents were not only well paid for them, but Fines frequently exacted; and we were not then over-burthen'd with Poor, as we are now; nor our Roads nor Streets infested with Highwaymen and Robbers: If the Rents for the Lands were then likewise well paid, and raised too, as they certainly were; and if now the Gentlemen can hardly get any Rents for their Lands; and all the contrary Marks and Signs are upon us: It must be plain that it is not the Plenty of the Produce, but too great a Scarcity of Money amongst the People, which hath reduced Trade to so languishing a Condition, that Tradesmen in general can't get Money to pay the usual Rents for the Houses, nor the Farmers for the Farms.

And this squares exactly with what I said to illustrate my fourth Principle, that if Money decreases amongst the People, they must be distress'd, unless either their Numbers be diminish'd, or the Prices of Things lower'd in such Proportion. And since these Marks and Signs are sufficient Proofs of too great

a Scarcity of Money amongst the People in general,
they must also be equal Proofs that the Cash
amongst them in general is considerably diminish'd,
at least that it is not increased in Proportion to
ıss their Number, and the Prices of Things. ‖

And hence we may see that whatever hurts Trade
to any considerable Degree, will also hurt the Landlords of Lands and Houses too, if there be any
Truth in the Fact contain'd in the Objection I have
now answer'd.

And if what I have offer'd be, as I think it is, a
sufficient Answer to the Objection, supposing the
Fact to be true, it follows then that the Gentlemen
if they would have any Rents for their Farms, are
under a Necessity, as fast as possible, to cause so
much waste Land to be inclosed and improved, as
shall actually reduce the present Rates of Labour,
and the Subsistence of the Farmers, so much, that
the Price, the Produce of the Earth will fetch at
Market, may be sufficient to bear all Charges, and
leave an Overplus to pay such Rents as the Lands
will then be found to bear. For whilst the necessary
Charges of the Labour, &c. and the Subsistence of
the Farmers continue so great, as to equal the Price
the Produce of the Ground fetches at Market, it is
impossible the Gentlemen should have any Rents
paid them.   The Objection suggests this to be the
Case at present; and I am sure that a Scarcity of
the Produce will not mend the Matter, whatever
they may think of such a Calamity.

Now that the necessary Charges of the Labour,
&c. and the Subsistence of the Farmers may be so
much lower'd, as to leave an Overplus out of the
Price the Produce of the Ground fetches at Market,
sufficient to pay some Rent, is certain; because,
when the Produce of the Ground did hardly fetch

₁₁ Part of its present Rates, some Rent was as certainly paid, as that ‖ we always had Gentlemen in ₁₅₉ the Kingdom who liv'd on their Estates. And if, as I have before sufficiently made out, the lowering the Rates of Labour will make every Thing fall, in much greater Proportion than the Rents, it must be evident that an Overplus must, in this Case, remain to pay Rent; and that the Gentlemen will be the richer too, for persuing such Measures, as shall be effectual to reduce the present Rates of Labour, &c. And now, I hope, it doth fully appear, that the Gentlemen have no Reason to fear improving so much waste Land as I am contending for, since perhaps they are not like to get any Rent any other way; except that I must add, that the taking the Taxes intirely off Goods, would mightily help them in this Point, since it's pretty certain, the Taxes, and Charges of collecting them, together with the Advance on the Price of Goods they occasion, do now absorb near half the Rent of the Kingdom, as hath been before shewn. Nay, I do verily believe, that taking the Taxes intirely off the Things the working People consume, is so absolutely needful, that Labour can hardly be reduced without it.

And that which makes me think so, is the prodigious Augmentation of the Price of Goods by Taxes; an undeniable Instance of which, the taking the Duty off Salt, and laying it on again hath produced. For Salt, when the Duty was taken off, was cried about Street three Pounds for five Farthings; and no sooner was the Duty laid on again, but the Price became to the Consumer (as it was before the Duty ‖ was taken off) five Farthings for one Pound. ₁₆₀ So that the Duty on Salt hath trebled its Price to the Consumer. This Instance therefore makes me think it impossible to reduce the Rates of Things

by Tillage, &c. alone, so much as to reduce the
Rate of Labour, except taking the Taxes intirely
off the Things the working People consume and use,
be also brought in Aid. And I dare say this will be
found so too, if ever it's tried.

But there remains a Difficulty or two, which perhaps it may also be needful to remove, *viz.*   First,
That since a great many Estates in this Kingdom
are mortgaged, if the Rents of Lands, by the Execution of this Proposal, should be considerably
lower'd, many such Estates will hardly be worth
more than they are mortgaged for; which may be
a very great Hardship to abundance of People.
I would therefore most humbly propose that, whenever the Wisdom of Parliament shall think fit to
make an Act to inclose, and improve so much common and waste Land as shall be needful, and may
be effectual to the Purposes this Essay sets forth;
(for I believe it can hardly be effected without such
an Act of Parliament;) I say, I would most humbly
propose, that a Clause be added, that all Mortgagees
shall be obliged annually, or in any other Manner
that may seem meet, to strike off such Sums from
the Principal Money lent on such Estates, as shall
hold Proportion to the Fall of the Rents of Lands.
This can be no Hardship to the Mortgagees, since
the Residue of their Money and Interest will do, at
161 least, all the same Things which their || whole Sums,
with the Interest, would have done if no such Alteration were made, as the full and sufficient Execution
of this Proposal will effect.

The Mortgagees will be so far from being singular
in this Case, that this is what must happen to every
Tradesman, whose Stock in Hand being our Produce, or Manufactures of any Kind, will be continually falling, as fast as such Produce or Manu-

factures shall from Time to Time, by the Plenty of them, be made cheaper. Nor will this be any Prejudice to any Tradesman, since every Time they buy, in this Case, such Goods will be as much cheaper than when they bought last, as those Commodities have fallen on their Hands; and the remaining Sums every way as powerful to buy what they may have Occasion for, as the whole Sums would have been if no such Alteration had happen'd, as this Proposal, if executed, will effect.

As to foreign Commodities, their Prices depending on the Markets whence they are brought, will hardly be affected by this Proposal; and as to Book Debts and Notes, the Credit of this Kind being never intended to be of any long Duration, I think no Alteration should be made, respecting them. But if this Proposal should be executed, a Hardship will fall on many who have Leases of Lands, unless a Clause be likewise made, to give such Tenants Leave to surrender their Leases to their Landlords; but this must only be at the Option of such Tenants, because if they think fit to hold their Leases, the Covenants must be fulfilled, even as || if no Alteration were 161 made by the Execution of this Proposal.

And if another Clause were made to this Purpose, that any Person being willing to inclose, and improve any reasonable and proper Quantity of waste Land, fit for one Person to undertake the Improvement of, wherever such waste or uninclosed Land is to be found,* such Person should have Power to do so, on Condition only of giving Notice in Writing to the Proprietors of such waste Land; or, if such

---

* Dr. *John Lawrence*, in his new System of Agriculture, *Page* 5, says, I can't but admire that the People of *England* should be so backward to enclose, which would be worth more to us than the Mines of the *Indies* to the King of *Spain*.

waste Land belong to a Parish, to the Vestry, who should receive* such Rents as shall be agreed by two Persons indifferently chosen, one by the Proprietors or Vestry, the other by the Incloser of such Lands: And if they can't agree, a third Person should be obliged to fix and determine the Rents for any proper Term: And it should be recommended by the same Act, that the Referees always have all due Regard to the Good of the Person inclosing and improving such waste Land, because the Riches, Strength, and Honour of a Nation depend on the utmost Improvements of their Lands, 163 all || other Things being only Consequences of this: I say, if such a Clause were further added, this whole Affair, and all the Benefits I have been representing, would thenceforth execute themselves, so long as we have any waste or unimprov'd Land left. And when we have no more, the People must remove themselves where they can have Land enough to support them; or our Country will certainly become weak and miserable, by its being more numerous, than the Continent we have can support in an happy Condition.

I shall conclude with offering something about the Execution of this Proposal. But shall premise, that since all Trade and Commerce is founded in the Wants of Mankind solely, and that these can be supplied only by Cultivation and Tillage, all other Things depending intirely thereon, it must

---

* The Rent paid to such Parishes or Vestries, should be annually distributed to those who had a Right of Commoning on such Lands as may, from Time to Time, be enclosed and improv'd; and that in such Proportion as their several Rights may intitle them to; unless the Parliament should think it more useful and beneficial to apply such Rents to the Relief of the Poor, in those and other Parishes that may stand in need of Assistance and Relief, or direct its Application any other fitter Way; or unless those who have the Right of Commoning, will enclose and improve it in such Parts, as their several Rights may intitle them to.

clearly appear to what Causes to attribute that Decay of Trade, of which such great Complaints have been made from all Parts of the Kingdom, even to the Parliament; and that those have not rightly consider'd the Nature and Foundation of Trade, who have so vilely traduced as wise and good a Government as this Nation ever had, when they have insinuated, at least, that this Decay of Trade is owing in any Degree to their Conduct.

For, I hope, I have shewn that a Decay of Trade will unavoidably arise from the Course of Things themselves, where such an Addition of Land is not annually cultivated, as shall at least hold Proportion to the natural Increase af Mankind; and likewise that a Decay ‖ of Trade is the necessary and un- 164 deniable Consequence of a Decrease of the Nation's Cash, since the Consumption of every Thing must lessen in such Degree, as the Cash circulating amongst the People lessens, if the Prices of Things in general be not reduced in like Proportion, by the Means I have shewn.

For if every Thing bears the same Price, and the Number of Consumers is not lessen'd, it's plain, they having in this Case so much less Money amongst them, must purchase as much fewer Things, as the Want of so much Money will necessarily prevent them from buying; and this will increase the Number of Poor, and make them miserable, according as the Degree of the Decrease of Cash cuts off more or less Business from amongst the People.

The Consequences will be just the same, if the People increase, and Cash doth not increase amongst them in like Proportion.

And further, I think it appears, that it is not Luxury which occasions a Decay of Trade; but

that such a Decay of Trade, as dispossesses many
of that Property their Wants and natural Rights
intitle them to, is that alone which possesses a com-
parative Few with such Affluence, as both causes
and supports their Luxury, and allures and draws
in many into such luxurious Excesses, as are beyond
their Abilities to support. Therefore, imputing the
Decay of Trade to Luxury, must be a very great
Error, since it puts the Effect for the Cause.

And again, I believe our Paper-Effects have con-
tributed as much to this Decay of Trade, as all the
165 rest put together, by inhancing the || Price of every
Thing amongst us, above the Rates our real Specie
would have supported them at, in such Proportion
as the Paper-Effects amongst us are greater than
the real Specie we have circulating; for this is the
natural and unavoidable Effect of any Thing operating as Cash, which is not such.

But to return: I would most humbly propose
that, if possible, 100,000 Acres of Land be for some
Years successively taken in, and inclosed, as near
London as such a Quantity of Land is to be had,
because the labouring People may, I believe, be
more easily drawn from hence to cultivate it, than
from any other Parts; and because the Cities of
London and *Westminster* will, I imagine, sooner feel
the Effects in the Cheapness of Provision of all
Kinds, which will soon put the Inhabitants into Circumstances to occupy more Houses, and cause
others to flow to them, and thereby fill the empty
Houses; for where the Trade is, the People will
come.

Again, I would most humbly submit it to the
Consideration and Goodness of His most Gracious
Majesty, whether his Majesty might not, by giving
his Crown Lands in proper Parcels on quit Rents,

or any proper Acknowledgments for a Term of
Years, begin this good Work, and relieve the poor
Artificers and Manufacturers, for whom His Majesty
hath from the Throne most graciously expressed
great Compassion.* ||

166

And if His most Gracious Majesty shall please
to continue to add, for some Years, such a Quantity
of Crown Lands, in several Parts of the Kingdom,
to be cultivated on like easy Terms, there will be
People enough that will accept and improve them.
And if at the End of any proper Term, when such
Possessors shall pay Rent for them, an Incouragement be given, by allowing such Parcels of Lands
on easy Rents, for some further Term of Years,
this Incouragement will be attended with the utmost
Improvement of such Lands, and Wealth to every
prudent and industrious Possessor of them, and will,
in a few Years, be a very considerable Estate to the
Crown, arising by these Rents; and hereby, the
dismal, and otherwise irremediable Calamity of
many will be alleviated and relieved, Tears wip'd
from many Eyes, and many broken Hearts heal'd,
and Multitudes saved from Imprisonment, Trans-
portation, and the Gallows; besides preventing
many from deserting the Kingdom, as they are now
continually doing, to seek that Bread, which they
can't find in their native Country, to support them
with Comfort.

Thus will His most Gracious Majesty become a
Kind of Deity to his People, whilst he is thus imi-
tating the Beneficence of our heavenly Father,
whose Representative on Earth he will thus be, in
the most exalted Sense.

---

* I look with Compassion upon the Hardships of the poor Artificers and
Manufacturers. See his Majesty's most Gracious Speech of *January* 13,
1729.

I must, indeed, own myself a Stranger to the
Quantity of Crown Lands, that are at present uncultivated; though I can't doubt that there are
enough to set this useful, and, as I believe, absolutely
167 needful Proposal at Work; which || will be found to
be an inexpressible Benefit to all Ranks and Degrees
of Men amongst us, if fully and sufficiently executed.

But I must further note, that if so great a Part of
the Kingdom as about 30000 square Miles, remain
at present uncultivated, as I have supposed in this
Essay, it will probably take more than one Century
to put it all to Use; so that there will be Land
enough to plant Timber on, beside what should be
raised in the Hedges and Banks.   For the making
Timber plenty, is undoubtedly of as great Importance to our Maritim Trade, and Naval Power, as
the Cultivation and Tillage, I have been contending
for, is to the Support and Happiness of the People;
beside the further Usefulness of such Plenty of Timber for Building, and making our Iron, tanning of
Leather, and many other Uses and Purposes, for
which it will become absolutely necessary, if ever
this Proposal should be executed.

But perhaps it may be thought, such an Addition
of Land every Year may reduce the Rents of Lands
too much.   In answer to which I shall only say that,
when the Necessaries of Life are reduced so low
that we can work as cheap as the Nations round
about us, and that the Wages of a working Man
will purchase enough to support such a Family, as
the Estimate is made for, in the Station of a labouring Man's Family; as none of them can then want
Work, which I think I have proved by shewing how
great the Wants of the People are; so the Rent
the Lands will then bear, is really that proper and
fit annual Rent, which || will be found best for all
168 Ranks and Stations of Men.

But if Things must not be put on so good a Foot,
I cannot help thinking, that it would be much happier
for the People, that they were in a State of Nature,
where all Men being born equal, have a natural
Right to any Quantity of Land they think fit to use,
and to put it to what Use they please, provided it be
not occupied by any other: For whoever occupies
any Land in this Case, is the rightful Possessor and
Proprietor, so long as he continues to occupy and
use it.   For though I don't think a State of Nature
to compare with the State of Civil Government, if
the Plenty be made great enough to support the
People comfortably, yet if the Bulk of Mankind be
made miserable by the Oppression of the rest; as
they undoubtedly are, when the Wages of the
Labourer, and Price of Necessaries for such a Family
as he must often sustain, and which indeed he was
chiefly sent into this World to raise, are not very
near equal: I say, such an unhappy State of Mankind is, in my Opinion, worse than a State of Nature
itself.

For as Men form themselves into Societies or
Governments, to make themselves more happy than
they would be in a State of Nature, it is but just,
that as they, for that End, give up their natural
Right to the Land, which by this Principle, that all
Men by Nature are born equal, they have an in-
defeasable Right to take and possess, wherever it
lies unoccupied by any other; I say, it is but just,
so much Land be continually added and improv'd
amongst ‖ them, that every Thing thereby be ren- 169
der'd so plentiful, and consequently so cheap, that
the Wages of the labouring Men, and Price of Necessaries become so equal, that they may all comfortably support such a Family, as they were sent
into this World to raise, and therefore ought to

support, unless through Sickness or Weakness such an one becomes unable to labour for them; and then his and his Family's Support becomes a just Debt on the Publick, so long as they really stand in need of it.

And, I further say, if so much Land were continually added, and so well improv'd as to keep these Points (*viz.* the Wages of the labouring Man, and Price of Necessaries for the Support of a Family) together, Trade could never stand in need of any other Care or Concern of any Government, let the Subjects carry it on in whatever Way or Manner they possibly could*. For if the Trade were so gainful, as to increase the Cash amongst the People, in greater Proportion than the People increase, the Prices of Things would only become higher in such Proportion. And if the Cash decreased (which, by the way, I believe would be impossible) as then more of the People must fall into Tillage, &c. from a Want of Business, which is the necessary Consequence of a much greater Importation of Foreign, than Exportation of our own Commodities; so || employing the People this Way, would bring down the Prices of Things to the Cash amongst them (*i. e.* to their proper Value), and would soon, by making their Produce and Goods so much cheaper, enable them to export more of their own, and import less foreign Goods, and thereby recover their foreign and maritime Trade.

Thus the Flux and Reflux of Trade, which we hence see is all govern'd by Money, or, in other

---

* This is the sole Rule concerning Trade, to which any Government should ever attend, and which, if sufficiently attended to, will always render them as powerful, and their People as happy, as the Nature of Things is capable of; and is therefore infinitely preferable to any Encouragements or Restraints in favour of Trade, which ultimately will always terminate in Mischief to Trade.

Words, by the Prices Goods of all Kinds bear in each Nation, with respect to the Prices of the same Kinds of Goods in each other Nation, would infallibly furnish as much Employment and Happiness, as the State of Mankind is capable of. And thus would Government answer up to the Felicity, Mankind wisely sought by uniting themselves into such Bodies and Societies. Nor could this possibly fail of making Mankind thus happy, unless the Defect be in the Constitution of the World it self to answer the End. And I think none, that have any just Sentiments of the Perfections of the Deity, will ever suppose that.

O happy Time! when shall it once be, that Princes and great Men of the World will let Mankind thus naturally employ, and make themselves happy! And by thus suffering them to support themselves, remove much of the Misery of the World, and together introduce Knowledge, and Prudence, and Virtue in much larger Degrees than at present! For Ignorance and Vice are almost inseparably connected with Poverty and Want. *The Destruction of the Poor is their Poverty.*

F I N I S.

NOTES

[1] (page 14)   Baker, Geoffrey-Le (d. 1358-60).   Chronicon Galfridi le Baker de Swynebroke [1303-56], ed. E. M. Thompson.   Oxford, 1889.— Another edition, J. A. Giles.   Caxton Soc. London, 1847.

[2] (page 23)   "A Conference with a Theist," in five parts, 8vo, 1696 (3rd edit., enlarged to 2 vols, in 1723).   For details of Nicholls's life as author and divine, see Dictionary of National Biography, *sub nom*.

[3] (page 35)   "Another Essay in Political Arithmetick, concerning the Growth of the City of London," 1683, p. 15 ; reprinted in " Economic Writings of Sir William Petty " (ed. Hull), p. 463.   Vanderlint's acquaintance with " Sir William Pettis's " opinions were probably derived, as intimated in the text, entirely from William Nicholls's " Conference with a Theist."

[4] (page 39)   August 20, 1714.

[5] (page 41)   October 19, 1711.

[6] (page 42)   " Physico-Theology : or, A Demonstration of the Being and Attributes of God, from His Works of Creation.   Being the substance of sixteen sermons preached in St. Mary-le-Bow-Church, London, at the Honourable Mr. Boyle's lectures, in the years 1711, and 1712.   With large notes, and many curious observations."   Eighth edition.   London, 1732. For the passage in question, see p. 176, note i.

[7] (page 44)   " New System of Agriculture, being a Complete Body of Husbandry and Gardening," 1726.   The author, John Laurence (not Lawrence, as p. 90, below), himself a clergyman, is best known for his " Clergyman's Recreation, shewing the Pleasure and Profit of the Art of Gardening," 1714—which reached a fourth edition in 1716 (Dictionary of National Biography, *sub nom*.).

[8] (page 45)   "A Treatise of Taxes and Contributions," 1662, p. 59 (Hull, p. 78); " The Political Anatomy of Ireland," 1691, p. 25 (Hull, p. 154); letter of Petty to Southwell, August 20, 1681 (Hull, p. 467).

[9] (page 48)   " The State of the Nation, in Respect to her Commerce Debts and Money."   London, 1725.   The author's name did not appear on the title-page, but was appended to the dedication " To the King." Modern interest in the tract, which was reprinted in 1726, in 1731 and in 1751, grows largely out of McCulloch's opinion that it contains at least one passage " not surpassed by anything in Smith or Ricardo " (" Literature of Political Economy," p. 351).

[10] (page 63) "State of Woolen Manufactures Considered." By Benjamin Ward, Yarmouth. Printed by R. Ford. 1731. 27 pp. 8vo. The author is not mentioned by McCulloch, Palgrave or the Dictionary of National Biography, but the tract is included in Massie's "Catalogue of Commercial Tracts," (No. 2801).

[11] (page 90) "Abridgement of the Royal Society's Transactions, from 1700 to 1720." 3 vols. 4to. London, 1721. Originally a printer, Motte developed into bookseller and publisher, and as such brought out "Gulliver's Travels," and other of Swift's writings (Dictionary of National Biography, *sub nom.*).

[12] (page 96) [Daniel Defoe], "A Plan of the English Commerce. Being a Compleat Prospect of the Trade of this Nation, as well the Home Trade as the Foreign." London, 1728. McCulloch notes that, "What is called the second edition is merely the first edition with a new title-page and a brief appendix" ("Literature of Political Economy," p. 45).

[13] (page 118) See p. 126 note, below.

[14] (page 130) May 11, 1713.

[15] (page 142) See note 8, above.

CPSIA information can be obtained
at www.ICGtesting.com
Printed in the USA
BVHW041721310721
613282BV00013B/447

9 781165 418916